THINGS OF DRY HOURS

Naomi Wallace

BROADWAY PLAY PUBLISHING INC
New York
www.broadwayplaypub.com
info@broadwayplaypub.com

THINGS OF DRY HOURS
© Copyright 2010 Naomi Wallace

Cover art: Bruce McLeod
First printing: September 2010
I S B N: 978-0-88145-454-3
Book design: Marie Donovan
Typographic controls: Adobe InDesign
Typeface: Palatino
Printed and bound in the U S A

THINGS OF DRY HOURS was originally commissioned by the Joseph Papp Public Theater/ New York Shakespeare Festival.

The play had its world premiere at Pittsburgh Public Theater (Ted Pappas, Artistic & Executive Director) on 15 April 2004. The cast and creative contributors were:

TICE.. Roger Robinson
CALI.. Rosalyn Coleman
CORBIN...Robert Sedgwick

Director...Israel Hicks
Scenic designer.. James Noone
Costume designer..Gabriel Berry
Lighting designer...Phil Monat
Composer & sound designer.............................. Fitz Patton
Dramaturg... Kyle W Brenton

THINGS OF DRY HOURS has also been produced in England at the Royal Exchange Theater and The Gate Theater, both productions directed by Raz Shaw. At Center Stage, the play was directed by Kwame Kwei-Armah.

THINGS OF DRY HOURS premiered in New York
in 2009 at New York Theater Workshop. The cast and
creative contributor were:

TICE .... Delroy Lindo
CALI .... Roslyn Ruff
CORBIN .... Garret Dillahunt

Direction .... Ruben Santiago-Hudson
Scenic design .... Richard Hoover
Costume design .... Karen Perry
Lighting design .... Marcus Doshi
Sound design & original music .... David Van Tieghem
Fight direction & effects design ....David Leong
Composer .... Bill Sims, Jr
Additional music .... Derek Wieland

CHARACTERS & SETTING

CALI HOGAN, *African-American woman, twenty-nine years old*

TICE HOGAN, *her father, mid to late fifties*

CORBIN TEEL, *white, mid to late thirties, Iowan*

Place: Small cabin near railroad line, Birmingham, Alabama.

Time: Early 1930s

Set: Minimal and not "realistic". A couple of chairs, a small, simple wood table, a stove.

Text: A break in the line by a period suggests a short beat, a half breath. Accents are mild.

This plays was inspired by Robin D G Kelley's book *Hammer and Hoe*. Without the brilliance of Kelley's work(s), I could not have written this story.

Special thanks to Peter Rachleff, whose research and notes towards this project were invaluable.

I'd like to thank Tera Hunter for the inspiration for Cali.

This play is for my children:
Nadira, Caitlin, and Tegan

Special thanks to Charles Isherwood for spurring me on.

We are things of dry hours and the involuntary plan.
Gwendolyn Brooks

Nothing that is worth doing can be achieved in our lifetime; therefore we must be saved by hope. Nothing we do, however virtuous, can be accomplished alone; therefore we are saved by love.
Reinhold Niebuhr

As long as you think you're white, there's no hope for you.
James Baldwin

ACT ONE

Prologue

(TICE *appears from another world. His shirt is untucked, suspenders hanging loose. He's come a long way.*)

TICE: Damn. Hope this is the right place. Well, it'll have to do 'cause I'm not about to make this trip twice. Fact is, I'm still warm. Though if I'd taken the time to get dressed, that little window, and you know what window I mean, would've come down with a bang and who knows when I'd've had another chance. (*Beat*) Strange thing is, there's no glass in that window. Whole things made of ice. The sill so cold when you put your knee up on it to climb through, your bones turn black with the shock. And then you just. Fall on through. And none of that slow motion elegant gliding through black nothingness either, but shot through the air like a raisin out the ass of a trumpeting elephant. Landing here. Still picking the crud of heaven out my ears like a new-born. Least I think it was heaven. Though I passed through so quick it could've been hell. On my journey here I saw three things: a chick-a-dee with a cow's tongue, a wheelbarrow hauling a city, and my own bare ass flashing by in the eye of a beetle. (*Beat*) There's something biblical there but I can't yet put my finger on it. I think it's the three.

Because I have come here, with such speed and
undignified travel, to speak with you about three
things:

One: the knock at the door. Because there is always a
knock at the door. And you know it's the knock at the
door that you've been telling yourself you haven't been
waiting for all your life, that it's just like yesterdays
knock on the door, or the day before. But this knock
is different. Not by its sound but by the way it opens
up a hole inside you and you start to cave in. And all
the while you're scrambling and scratching to hold on
inside, you're getting up, real calm, and going to the
door to open it. Two: the nature of apples. For if you
eat enough apples and save the seeds, which I did,
and which is no easy thing because they're small and
slippery little bastards, you might begin to wonder:
how many seeds does it take to fill the human hand?

Three: The good friend. A good friend does not fit in
the human hand. A good friend does not knock at the
door. A good friend is not a dinner plate, nor a piece
of string. Is a good friend an apple seed? Imagine the
treasures a man toys with in a lifetime. Now close your
eyes. But watch the back of your lids 'cause what I saw
in my short time was not what I held in my arms; what
I spoke was not the weight I felt on my tongue; what
I touched I touched in the dark even when the world
was lit up as bright as a furnace.

And it is 1932. In Birmingham, Alabama. And the
world is a furnace. For while the fat of the fire drips
down the monstrous chins of a few small pale gods,
iron ore workers, steel workers, coal miners, black and
white, are out of work, out of world. National Guard
shoot diamonds into the backs of strikers in the park.
The Red Cross waves cold pistols over angels on relief
as the Share Croppers Union smokes in gun battles
with police. Boweevils grow so fat they use them

for tires and judases bloom. *And all the while, T C I,*
Tennessee Coal and Iron, cathedral of steel and smoke,
leans down over the city's crib from all directions and
smothers her in her sleep. Sidewalks are beaten 'til
they are unrecognisable 'cause they won't get up off
the street. And even the black elite turns its back on
a morning that refuses to come back some other day.
And the birds. The birds are so thin with hunger you
can use them for a book mark. If you can catch them.
If you have a book. And I do. I, Tice Hogan, have two
books. And I am alive to all things that bind us. *(He*
buttons up his shirt and adjusts his suspenders as he speaks
the following:) I am a teacher at a local Sunday school.
I sing in the choir at my church. I eat apples and save
the seeds. And I pay my two cents a month dues as a
member and unit leader of the Communist party of
Alabama. Hallelujah.

(End Prologue)

Scene One

(Stillness. TICE *stands reading a small book. A splitting log*
rolls onto the stage, slowly, and comes to rest in the room.
He regards it, but then returns to reading. After a moment,
a smaller log rolls in after it and comes to a rest. Stillness.
Then CALI *appears with an ax.* CALI's *shoes don't quite*
match, but she wears them well)

CALI: It's not Saturday today.

TICE: I believe it is.

CALI: No. It's Friday.

TICE: Could be Thursday.

CALI: You know its not. It's Friday today and denying
that, denies the Lord.

TICE: Watch your self, girl. The Lord lets slip the days of the week, but not the weak of the tongue.

CALI: Is it preaching time already? Must be Sunday now.

TICE: Be quiet. I'm reading. Are you reading?

CALI: No. I'm swingin' an ax. This was your Friday to do it. Last Friday was too.

(CALI *watches* TICE *a few moments, then she picks up the smaller log, places it on the larger, and picks up the ax. He doesn't look at her as he speaks, but focuses on his book*).

TICE: Don't do that in here, girl. It'll bring us bad luck.

CALI: You don't believe in luck.

TICE: That's cause luck never believed in me.

(CALI *swings the ax and splits the wood in one easy motion. Now Tice looks at her*)

TICE: Arms are getting thick, girl. That's good. Strong. Men don't like it. But you're never one to care.

CALI: Guess what I found in one of the sheets today?

TICE: *(Back to his book)* A lady's slipper. A gentleman's belt.

CALI: A blue ribbon. Look. *(She has a blue ribbon in her hair)*

TICE: Stealing's—

CALI: A sin. And it's this little bit of sin that reminds me to be good.

TICE: But the colour is not for you, it's too...

CALI: I'm keepin' it.

TICE: All right. Then write a letter. Ask instead of steal. Write: Could I have the ribbon that I found in your sheet?

CALI: I won't ask for anythin' but my pay.

TICE: How would Marx consider this situation?

CALI: He'd say if you find a ribbon when you're washing out their soil, then take it and wear it.

TICE: No. He'd say save your resistance for the larger battles. Stealing ribbons is not one of them. Now, if you took to smuggling some of our flyers in those sheets like your good friend Estelle does—

CALI: I won't work for your party.

TICE: Well. A dead husband will not notice a ribbon anyway.

CALI: My husband may be dead but his eyes are open. Always did like to watch the world. But he doesn't need a fire to do it. You're the one who needs the fire day and night.

TICE: Daughter, I'm reading.

CALI: My arms are thick? Your arms? Out of work. You used to have steel for arms. Look at yourself. That's what reading a book so long does to a man: thins the muscle. A bird could land on your arm just like a wire.

TICE: You need some air, my daughter. It's Friday night. Go on down to the Joy Boy club and dance with the girls. Do some fast foot. Shake out that sag. Look at the men. You're not old yet.

CALI: Old enough to know that one's the same as the next.

TICE: Find one and change him. Fix him just like you like it.

CALI: Stones don't change.

TICE: A man is not a stone.

CALI: I'm not talkin' about a man. I'm talkin' about me.

TICE: No, no. You're wrong, girl. It's happening all the time. Even inside of you. Me, look what I've molded myself into? I couldn't even sing as a child and now: *(He lets out a couple of beautiful lines of song from his choir)* Top of the choir. Sometimes I even think if you just look at a thing long enough it'll change, just out of spite. Sit down. I'll read to you.

CALI: From which book?

TICE: Does it matter?

CALI: I've got to finish stacking wood. Soup for dinner.

TICE: Unit meeting at Tucker's house tonight. Getting a block relief committee together to push for cash wages, 'stead of scrip. The six of us. I might sing, too. You can come.

CALI: I've got work.

TICE: Unlike the women and men that'll be there. Relief projects started on the new Park. But only for scrip.

CALI: Don't start.

TICE: No cash, forced to shop at high priced shops—

CALI: Here, take this ribbon and give it to your lowest unemployed. *(She takes the ribbon from her hair and gives it to her father)*

TICE: You make me sad 'cause you're not happy.

CALI: I don't ask to be happy. Be happy for that. I just want to be left alone. Here with you. It's all right. The world's out there. Hungry, it can stay there.

TICE: Things could be different.

CALI: Old man. Now you make me sad.

TICE: The party could put a skip in your step.

CALI: I don't need a skip in my step.

TICE: Why won't you listen to me?

CALI: A skip in my step?

TICE: Or a swing in your swoop? A man in your hand?

CALI: Father.

TICE: A spark in your bark?

CALI: There's nothing wrong with my step. If you keep out of the way.

(End Scene One)

Scene Two

(TICE is reading his huge bible. CALI enters with a basket of unfolded sheets. She begins to fold the sheets and stack them on the chair)

CALI: You know what Rosie says about men with enormous bibles?

TICE: Nope, and neither do I want to hear it from my daughter. Rosie doesn't think, let alone talk like that. Not about me anyway. *(He focuses on his bible as he speaks)*

CALI: She does.

TICE: She doesn't.

CALI: No, she doesn't.

TICE: She doesn't, really?

CALI: No, but she was round here earlier, lookin' all biblical and ready for some Sunday schoolin'...

TICE: What did she say? She doesn't say much so what she does say will be significant.

CALI: I wonder if I could have some sugar, Cali girl. That's all she said.

TICE: Well, it stands to reason.

CALI: You're disappointed.

TICE: I'd have to have some expectations to be disappointed. I don't have any expectations regarding—

CALI: But she did look all around here and it weren't for sugar since I had that covered.

(CALI *exaggerates Rosie, enjoying tormenting her father.*)

CALI: She looked all around as if searchin', sniffin' even.

TICE: Sniffing?

CALI: And her mouth all open.

TICE: Open?

CALI: With expectation. Kind of. A mouth open as if waitin' to be filled by—

TICE: For the final time, I know where you're going and I don't want to hear such things. Not from my daughter.

CALI: A man carryin' that isn't going anywhere in a hurry.

TICE: But you forget the other book. Made for travelling.

CALI: So ditch the heavyweight.

TICE: A Sunday school teacher must know his students. And these two books agree on a number of points.

CALI: Do unto others as you would have them do unto you.

TICE: Number one rule, and if we'd all do unto others-

CALI: And that gets us right back to Rosie

(TICE *begins humming so as not to hear* CALI.)

and what she wants to do unto you and—

TICE: Those sheets always do this to you, I swear.

CALI: And what you want to do unto her except you're too big a coward.

TICE: Now you know I've tried my share of women over the years. Just didn't work out.

CALI: Rosie, Rosie, Rosie.

TICE: I'm not listening any further.

CALI: Offering you her sugar posy.

TICE: I'm not listening.

CALI: You're dryin' up into a set of words, all marching along a straight and narrow road.

TICE: If I'm marching it's to a tune your mother first put in my ear. When justice gets ahold of you like that—wrapped up in your ear drum—you can't ever let it go.

CALI: And Rosie? And her posy?

TICE: What with the party, the Sunday teaching, the choir, couple days a week digging for the park, my days and much of my nights are stuffed to bursting and then...there's you and me. We fill my space just fine.

CALI: What, I got to go for you an' taste Rosie's sugar posy?

TICE: I come home to relax. You're running me into the ground with this Rosie business.

(CALI *picks up the basket of sheets but doesn't move*)

TICE: What now?

(CALI *just waits*)

TICE: Okay. I won't mention a husband again. You made your point.

(CALI *smiles and leaves with the laundry*)

TICE: (*Chants quietly to himself as he reads*) Rosie, Rosie, Rosie, offering her sugar posy.

(*End Scene Two*)

Scene Three

(*It is night.* TICE *is asleep in a chair, his huge bible on his lap. Two short, sharp knocks are heard. He stirs but doesn't wake.* CALI *enters in her sleeping-gown, alert, and listens for some moments. Then all is silent. She is uncertain if she heard anything. She returns to her father.*)

CALI: You asleep?

(TICE *does not stir.*)

CALI: That's good.

(CALI *carefully removes the Bible from* TICE's *arms. She tears out a page, slowly, so it makes an eerie sound.* TICE *sleeps on.*)

CALI: Forgive me Father for I have sinned. (*She tears out another page, but in short bursts so it tears differently*) Twice so far. Here goes a third. (*She tears out a third page in a different manner from the other two*) That's a kinder music, Lord. He won't know it cause he only goes to his earmarked pages. When he wakes he won't be missin' somethin' he doesn't know he had. (*Beat*) And I need it to wipe 'cause he won't let me use the party newspaper. (*She puts the torn pages into her pocket, then stands over her father*) I'm goin' to bed. You still asleep? (*She lightly brushes his hair once, but doesn't want to wake him.*) Still a handsome man. But I can't remember her like you do cause I was only six but she must of loved you up 'til you couldn't stand it anymore. Because you never seemed to need to find it again. What was it like, Daddy, to be loved like that?
    I lied to you. My husband's eyes are not open in his

grave. They were closed when he lived and closed when he died. He never could bear to look at me. I mean, really look at me. You ever have a hand touch you like it was touchin' a table, or reachin' for a bowl of soup? Then you'd know me.

(There is another knock at the door. After some moments someone knocks again. The knocks are short and precise, not desperate. TICE *wakes and listens. Another knock.* CALI *and her father look at one another. They are both afraid. The knocks sound again).*

CALI: *(Whispers)* Should we see who it is?

TICE: It's after midnight.

CALI: *(Calls)* Who's out there?

TICE: *(Louder)* Who's out there?!

(No answer)

CALI: Maybe they're gone.

TICE: They raided Kelley's place last night. Found a newspaper under the floor. Beat him and his two boys.

CALI: You never said.

TICE: The other night, it was Sumner's. Hit his wife too. Broke her jaw. Every third house in the district, police went in swinging hard. *(Again, three knocks)*

CALI: *(Firmly)* Daddy, there's no body out there.

TICE: That's right. There's no body out there.

CALI: So let's get some rest.

TICE: Won't be able to sleep now. I'll just sit the night out.

CALI: Don't open that door. It's just the wind.

TICE: The wind. Yeah.

CALI: Call me if you need me.

*(*CALI *exits.* TICE *tries to sleep)*

(End Scene Three)

Scene Four

(Bright early morning. CALI *enters with a basket and dumps a dozen single shoes on the floor. There are men's shoes, ladies' slippers, a child's sandal. None of the shoes match.* TICE *wakes. He's hardly slept)*

TICE: What the hell time is it?

CALI: Time for another pair of shoes. I've got almost nine months worth here.

*(*CALI *sits on the floor and begins to sort the shoes. She lines them up in front of her)*

TICE: You stay in this house today. Whoever was at the door last night might be waiting for us to leave.

CALI: Then I'll wack him with my shoe.

TICE: Cali. This is no joke.

CALI: I can crack a nut with the heel. Or kill a wasp. *(She smacks the shoe heel down hard on the floor)* I can pop a skull if I have to. Stop worrying!

TICE: Cali, Cali, Cali. How do so many shoes end up lost in those sheets you gather and wash?

CALI: People are careless.

TICE: But why careless with only one shoe? Why not with both?

CALI: Careless by half. And in some ways, that's worse than by full. Because when you lose one shoe in the laundry, you're not even tryin'. I can't stand folks with half measures.

TICE: Then why keep them?

CALI: Because I do like shoes. *(She picks up a shoe and studies it)* A child's slipper. This is a sad child. See how the toe has pushed down and made a dent. This is a child that holds onto the ground, afraid of being blown away. And this one *(A man's bedroom slipper)*. A cold man, and selfish. There's no imprint in the slipper. He can't hardly relax. Jealous the heat in his foot will leave him. Probably by the name of Mister George. *(A ladies shoe)* Oh I won't wear this one. Something bad happened here. A stain on the toe.

TICE: Blood?

CALI: Worse.

TICE: What could be worse?

CALI: Sorrow.

TICE: Sorrow doesn't stain.

CALI: Some kinds do. Here *(another man's shoe. Cali puts it on her hand like a puppet, and makes up a voice for it)*

CALI: *(Voice of the shoe)* I'm still warm inside. Happiness makes you hot. *(She nears TICE with the shoe as it talks.)* You don't believe me? *(She puts the shoe near TICE's face.)* Touch my seams, they're so hot they're burnin'.

TICE: I don't like it when you do this.

CALI: *(Voice of the shoe)* You don't like it when I do this? Kiss it.

(TICE doesn't respond. Now CALI turns the "puppet" to her own face and talks to herself)

CALI: *(Voice of the shoe)* Kiss it, you whore.

(CALI puts the tip of the shoe in her mouth. For one moment she lets it sit there, then TICE slaps it away to the ground. They are silent some moments.)

TICE: Three hundred other men like me laid off the steel works. If I had that job back, you could quit. You ever let them touch you?

CALI: Seen a worse shoe than this happy shoe. *(Beat)* Touched my neck, my shoulder, as I was carryin' the sheets out. But I kept movin'. Turnin'. Just a few steps ahead. Then out the door. Not this time. No. Not this time. Hey, I've been thinkin' 'bout your revolution.

TICE: Thank the Lord.

(CALI takes off one of her own shoes and uses it to talk to the other one.)

CALI: And the situation now, before we get the changes, when one of them touches me I say

CALI: *(Voice of the shoe)* Oh, please don't, sir. I have to hurry. Scurry. Worry. No offence but please just don't. Just please, please don't. *(Her own voice)* But when we get those changes, there's only one thing I'm waitin' for: *(Voice of the shoe)* Oh, please don't, sir. *(She changes her voice to reflect a new attitude)* I say. Don't. And if you ever touch me again I'll rip that shoe lace right out of your mouth, wrap it 'round your tongue and tie your seems up so tight that if you so much as breathe on me again I'll just go 'pling,' 'pling' and your plug will drop right off.

TICE: Always been a barefoot man, myself. Never really liked to be in shoes.

(CALI takes off her other shoe. As she speaks, she puts on the discarded man's shoe, then sorts through the other shoes until she finds a size that fits. She puts these two odd shoes on. They are different shoes but fit well.)

CALI: Ah, but a different set of shoes will take you the last place you knew you wanted to go. Might not change ourselves, but we can sure change where we're going. *(CALI looks down at her odd but new shoes and does a couple of dance steps with them.)* What do you think? Where will they take me?

(There is a sharp knock at the door. TICE and CALI freeze.)

CALI: Father. Lets open the door.

(TICE *regards* CALI, *then nods.* CORBIN *suddenly appears. He is dishevelled, dirty and uncertain. He gains confidence as the scene progresses.*)

CORBIN: My name is Corbin Teel.

(*Silence between the three of them*)

CORBIN: There was a ruckus at the foundry. A fellow caught up with me said you could help me. Hide me out. That you, Tice Hogan, were with the Party.

TICE: What fellow?

CORBIN: Didn't give his name. Just yours.

TICE: I can't help you, sir.

CORBIN: Just a few days.

TICE: I'm not with the Party. Dirty reds. Not my style, sir.

CORBIN: His name was Clyde Johnson. Worked beside me. He saw what happened, gave me your name.

TICE: Clyde Johnson? Never heard of him. I'm sorry.

CORBIN: I've got nowhere to go. They'll string me up if they catch me.

CALI: (*Quietly*) No, Father.

CORBIN: Fact is. I hit a man.

TICE: How hard?

CORBIN: He's the foreman.

TICE: With what?

CORBIN: Tennessee Coal and Iron.

TICE: You hit him with what?

CORBIN: With a stick.

TICE: A stick.

CORBIN: Three inch wide.

TICE: Did he get back up?

CORBIN: Of iron. They closed down two more blast furnaces. Foreman was layin us off. At random. He picked me. No reason. I hit him, then ran.

TICE: Clyde Johnson doesn't work at the foundry.

(CORBIN *enters the room a couple more steps. He has a slight limp.*)

CORBIN: You're right. It wasn't Johnson who talked to me. I got his name from the fellow who sent me.

TICE: And his name you can't remember.

CORBIN: He said this fellow he knew, Clyde Johnson, said you might help me.

CALI: My father is no Red.

CORBIN: (*To* TICE) I don't care what you are. I've got no money, no place to hide. (*He notices the pile of shoes on the floor.*) No decent shoes.

TICE: Too dangerous. They find you here, T C I police. They're more law than the law.

CALI: They'd kill us all.

CORBIN: A couple nights. I'll stay hid.

TICE: Let me be frank.

CORBIN: No one saw me come here.

TICE: Firstly, you're of a white persuasion so we can't be in the same house.

CORBIN: This fellow swore you'd help me—

TICE: Secondly, I can risk my own life if I take you in, but not my daughter's.

CORBIN: He said.

TICE: You have to leave. Immediately. Please.

CORBIN: *(Continues)* —that if you didn't help me, I was to tell you that I'd go turn myself in to the police and then get leniency by saying you, Tice Hogan, put me up to attacking the foreman because *(He makes a slow and carefully remembered list)* you are a dirty, red, crime-animal anarchtic,—

TICE: That'd be "criminal anarchist".

CORBIN: Free-leaving,

TICE: "Free-loving"

CORBIN: foreign born, exploding Jew

TICE: exploiting

CORBIN: Exploiting Jew, feeding off colored ignorance and excavating lurid sex

TICE: Advocating

CORBIN: Advocating lurid sex between...Negroes

TICE: Niggers

CORBIN: Yeah, and white women. *(Beat)* And all those things, you're daughter too, *(Turns to* CALI*)* pleased to meet you, Ma'am.

(CORBIN holds out his hand and keeps it there, but CALI does not take it.)

(End Scene Four)

Scene Five

(The next morning. CORBIN has slept on the floor. TICE comes in with a bowl of hot cereal and sits to eat breakfast. He doesn't look at CORBIN. He sips his cereal. CORBIN stands up and begins to inch his way over to the table.)

CORBIN: Mornin'.

(TICE answers with a long slurp.)

CORBIN: Floor's all right. Kind of soft, almost. I appreciate it.

(TICE *begins to scrape with his spoon.*)

CORBIN: I'd pay you board but I got no money. Had some. Not much. A drink. A knuckle of bread. They say you're for the workin' man, colored and white. Speakin' for the jobless, organizin' for work relief. That the Party's the only place in Birmingham where men like me and you sit at the same table. Where the colored man can speak against the white man if he's done wrong, even kick him out the Party if he acts with disrespect. No other place like that. Well I'm jobless now. I was loading coal at T C I. Beside men like you. Never got high up. Before that, button cutter in Muscatine. Iowa. That's where I was born. Cutting buttons from Mississippi river mussel shells. You got a shirt with buttons. I might of made one of those buttons. Ever been in a button cuttin' room? The shells give off a fine white dust that don't settle. You walk out after your shift and you're covered in it. Just like snow. Even in August. Forty men coming off our shift at midnight like an army of snowmen. In the heat. Hard times hit, they dumped our wages, over and over 'til the money they put in my hand. Well. (*He holds his empty hand out*) Added up to that. But I still hung on. Signed a yellow-dog contract, fixed rate, said yes to no union. But we got laid off anyhow. Then on down here to Alabama. Second day in the mines a man next to me puts his pickax in my thigh right to the bone. That's where I got my limp. But I never lost a day of work in that mine. 'Til they laid us off. You ever hear a pickax hit the bone? (*Makes a sound of the pick in the bone*) There's some of us, they work. Others of us, they look like they work. Can't hardly tell the difference. But I can.

(TICE *has finished his cereal. He takes the bowl and spoon
and taps them together, like he's applauding* CORBIN'*s
effort.*)

TICE: Not bad. How 'bout this: First day, steel plant,
twenty three years ago. I was just shoving sand,
pushing boards, but the second day on the floor:
molding. I had my own floor, twelve feet wide, twenty
feet long. I set my molds in a row, my walkway
between the molds. They showed me everything, how
to make the sand, how to line my mold. It was a first-
class skilled job, molding. I was making a four inch tee
and a 4 inch ell. It was heavy work, paid by the mold.
Not paid much. But I was goood. And that's good
spelled with three o's when two isn't enough. But I
wasn't a road man. That's a hot-shot fellow who can
put up more molds than the average man. That was Joe
Holton. Now he was a road man.

CORBIN: White?

TICE: Nah. And he wasn't full of muscle but he had
arms weren't made of bone. No, what run through
Holton's flesh was steel pipe, that strong. Every dip
was a ladle of molten iron, and that ladle held sixty
pounds of metal. Carrying that sixty pounds one
hundred times or more. *(Whistles his admiration).* But
Holton was a drinker, went to blind pigs and bought
bootleg whiskey. He started a tall man. Months pass,
carrying that load, and Holton's bent over, half my
size. And he keeps getting shorter until one day he
dropped one of those ladles right where we were
stood to dip. I jumped up out of the way. Holton, he
was left standing in it until both his feet were gone.
Then he just fell over. Not like a man, but a piece of
wood. I carried him out of the foundry. I laid him in
the little bit of grass they got left outside the plant. He
opened his eyes then. He said "What day is it?" I said
"Tuesday." He said "Are my feet gone?" I said "Yeah,

Joe Holton. Your feet are gone." He smelled sweet.
of whiskey and burning. Holton said "Look up there,
Tice. Look at all that sky." And we both looked up and
I never saw it so blue in that minute, never did again.
Joe said "I do believe I'm going to heaven, Tice. But
ain't it a shit when I get there with no feet I'm gonna
have to crawl." *(Beat)* I will feed you, Mr. Teel.

CORBIN: Please, call me Corbin.

TICE: But not much. Been out of work a long time
myself now. Do a couple days a month on the relief
project building the city park, but paid in scrip, not
cash. Pick up a little teaching on Sundays.

CORBIN: I've got a stomach the size of a dime.

TICE: I'll keep you safe 'cause I got no choice. Sit down.
I will come and go in this house—

CORBIN: Nice house.

TICE: House belongs to the church. Half dozen up the
road do too.

CORBIN: Good chair. Sturdy.

TICE: You'll stay put, lay low, keep quiet. I'll tell folks
I've got a sick cousin laid up with greenlung fever.
That way none of the neighbors'll dare come near this
house. But in one week, you will leave. *(Beat)* Why'd
you come to this house?

CORBIN: A man who thinks like you, workin on that
park. I don't get it. That's gonna be a whites- only park.

TICE: It's work. And it gives me a chance to talk to
other men like me.

CORBIN: You mean it gives you a chance to... recruit.
That what you call it?

TICE: My daughter can fill this bowl. Almost like a
miracle. Doesn't taste much like porridge, what Cali
makes. And her soup, damn. We grow and swap

vegtables with our neighbors but it must be something criminal she does with those potatoes. That fine. *(Beat)* One week, and then you leave. Do we have an agreement?

(CORBIN *looks hungrily at* TICE's *bowl, then at* TICE)

CORBIN: One week. Yeah. We can shake on it.

(CORBIN *holds out his hand.* TICE *doesn't take it, and exits.)*

(End Scene Five)

Scene Six

(CORBIN *is doing nothing, bored.* CALI *enters, carrying a bucket of underwear and socks to wash. She begins to wash the laundry on a scrub board.* CORBIN *studies her. She does not look at him when he speaks)*

CORBIN: Outside is where my mother did the laundry. More room, keeps the floor dry.

(CALI *continues with her work, ignoring him.)*

CORBIN: Smells nice. The soap does. Not a lot of that around. Where'd you get it? Haven't used that kind of soap in... Shouldn't say. Too good to use on laundry. Behind my ears, I feel a callin'. *(Beat)* I thank you for the soup you been feedin' me. You made it. Lots of folks out there with nothin' in their mouths. Ma'am, it'd be nice if you'd speak to me. Your father. Doesn't really speak to me. More like 'at'. Still, those folks are outside, doin'. I'm stuck here, not doin'. Rather do laundry. Though I'm a man. *(He starts to move closer.)*

CALI: I can handle this on my own, sir. Thank you.

CORBIN: Well.

CALI: It's what my father wants.

CORBIN: Say that again.

CALI: It's what my father wants.

CORBIN: No. The other word.

CALI: Which word?

CORBIN: The small one.

(CALI *doesn't understand* CORBIN.)

CALI: Sir?

CORBIN: That's it. Say it again.

CALI: Why, sir?

CORBIN: I like it. Haven't heard that said. To me, anyway, in a while. From a woman.

CALI: Any man in this house not my father is 'sir' to me.

CORBIN: Why're you doin' the laundry in here, not out back?

CALI: Just keepin an eye on the house.

CORBIN: Oh. *(Beat)* You think I'd steal from your father?

CALI: Don't know you. Might be a good man.

CORBIN: Thank you.

CALI: Might not. No offence, sir. We aren't starvin. My father's got a little money stored up. I wash. Some there too. Keep it well hid, but still.

CORBIN: I never stole from friends.

CALI: We are not your friends, sir.

CORBIN: Put a roof over my head, food in my gut, that's friend to me.

CALI: You said you'd turn us in for putting you up to a killin'.

CORBIN: I didn't kill anyone.

CALI: The man you hit never got back up.

CORBIN: Maybe he did after I was gone.

CALI: Maybe he didn't.

CORBIN: I get the distinct feelin' you don't like me.

CALI: You threatened my father so he'd take you in.
Me, I'd a taken you in, then while you slept, run a fork
through your gut, dragged you out back of the railroad
and dumped you. No one would miss you. Not your
kind. Sir.

CORBIN: My kind.

CALI: Lotsa men around like you. Born with little. Die
with less. Sir.

CORBIN: You'da murdered a man in his sleep?

CALI: Best way to do it.

CORBIN: You're pulling my leg.

CALI: Got a long fork. Length of my arm I use in the
fire.

CORBIN: You're not a killer. *(Beat)* Where those socks
from?

CALI: Shades Valley. Sheets from Mountain Brook
Estates.

(CORBIN whistles)

CORBIN: Washin for the finest families in Alabama.
(Beat) You don't know me. Shouldn't dislike a man you
don't know. You want me to help you.

CALI: Men don't wash socks, sir.

CORBIN: Reds say a new kind of man comin' out of this
decade.

CALI: We are not Reds. And there's no such thing as
a new kind of man. Please. Go sit and be quiet, sir. I
want to tell my father when he gets back that all you've
done all day is sit and be quiet.

CORBIN: You're not with the Party?

CALI: No.

CORBIN: Swear to God.

CALI: I swear to God.

(CORBIN *makes up the following as he goes along.*)

CORBIN: ...Reds say...in this new world, the women and the men, they'll work side by side. As equals. They'll kneel down over. The bucket of dreams. And that bucket's full of. Soapy water and there they'll wash the socks.

CALI: Reds say that.

CORBIN: Yeah, what I hear. But folks won't be washin' the socks from Shades Valley, but their own socks and their neighbours, in good yarn, no darned heels, and each person'll have three pairs of socks. Two wool, one cotton for summer. Not a bad world. If it could be like that.

CALI: Hmmm. And in this new world, who will work and who will sit and gabble?

(CORBIN *making it up as he goes.*)

CORBIN: They say. Everyone will do a bit of both. And work will be from dawn 'til dusk, but slow and lots of water to drink in between the hours. And the old will play with the children. The young will labor. And sing. Oh. And there's a little song Mister Red himself wrote:
(Sings)
Stand up from the bucket, come away from the steel
They've broken our backs, but not our hard will.

(CALI *looks at* CORBIN *for the first time now and frowns. He tries again*)

CORBIN: *(Sings)*
Wash only the socks that the laborer wears
and the water all 'round us will clean up our...cares.

CALI: *(Not even smiling)* And what is it you yourself believe about this "new" world? Sir.

CORBIN: The thing I believe in? *(Turns away)* That we're all gonna die. One way or another. No matter whose socks we wash.

(End Scene Six)

Scene Seven

(TICE enters with a plate of dried meat and begins to eat. CORBIN seems to be waiting for him.)

CORBIN: Where'd you go tonight? To a meeting?

(TICE ignores him.)

CORBIN: What'd you talk about?

(TICE just eats.)

CORBIN: The meetings are mixed, right? How many are white? Hell. How do you expect to recruit folks when you won't even talk to them? I'm stuck up in here day and night. Your daughter doesn't like me. One bowl of porridge in the morning. A splash of soup at night. My buttons are getting lost in my ribs I'm that lean. Look, I can see the crime in making folks work for nothing. I don't like the way things are. I might even work to make a change. But if you won't let me in, talk to me. Tell me how it goes.

(TICE chews on.)

CORBIN: I give you my word.

TICE: For what?

CORBIN: For anything.

TICE: Why?

(CORBIN starts to speak but TICE shushes him.)

TICE: Nah. Not that hogsloggin-gobbledygook you've been talking. Try it again. Convince me. Why should I accept your word?

(CORBIN *takes a moment to think this over.* TICE *helps him along.*)

CORBIN: Because I need...

TICE: a new...

CORBIN: Way...

TICE: Direction.

CORBIN: Yeah. A new direction. All my life I thought the dirt was passing under my heel as I walked, that I was...

TICE: Covering ground.

CORBIN: That I was coverin' ground. But it's the ground thats been moving, not me. You could change that. You could give me...

TICE: A map?

CORBIN: Exactly.

TICE: I don't trust you. So why should I take the risk?

CORBIN: Because you want to.

TICE: All right.

(CORBIN *lets out a whoop, then shuts himself up.*)

CORBIN: So when's the next meeting?

TICE: I like a challenge. Even your kind.

CORBIN: You don't even know my kind.

TICE: That's where you're wrong. Just never have them in my house.

CORBIN: You might learn somethin'.

TICE: Think so? Well. You like to read?

CORBIN: No. I don't.

TICE: Good. Then we'll start with reading.

CORBIN: Don't like reading. It stings my eyes.

TICE: We'll start with reading and we'll keep with reading until you love it. Until your face looks like a page.

CORBIN: Your face don't look like a page.

TICE: Now, choose your book. I've got two books. This big one here and this little one. You can choose which one to read.

CORBIN: What's the big one?

TICE: The big one is the Lord's Holy bible.

CORBIN: I'll study this little one then. What is it?

TICE: The manifesto of the communist party.

CORBIN: Shit.

TICE: That's what I thought 'til I began to read it. *(He hands it to* CORBIN.*)* There's only three copies in all Birmingham. Be careful with it. Go on. Have a look inside.

*(*CORBIN *opens the book. He studies the first page.)*

CORBIN: I don't know.

TICE: Niether did I. First big meeting I went to in Birmingham. 'Bout seven hundred colored folk, maybe a hundred whites. At Capitol Park, protesting the arrests of six fine communists in Atlanta. To the left of me, Hosea Hudson, champion of the Scottsburo boys: the man sweats justice. To the right of me, an old woman, jumping up and down and calling with the vigour of a child. And suddenly I was breathing deep. And I mean God deep. I'd always been a bible man and I grew up in church, but I never stood in a crowd like that. We were shouting for work relief, shouting 'gainst segregation. But it wasn't just the words that

took me up. It was a kind of. Humming. All those
bodies together, yearning in that hot May sun. I've
held women in my arms, yeah. And my own child. But
it was the first time I didn't feel. Alone.

CORBIN: Almost a miracle, huh?

TICE: Almost.

(CORBIN *hands the book back to* TICE.)

CORBIN: I'll be straight with you. I'm going to be a hard
case. I don't believe in it.

TICE: Don't believe in what?

CORBIN: Communist thoughts. Ways. Doings. I'm for
keeping it simple.

TICE: This book is very simple. You said you wanted a
map. This book is a map.

(TICE *now holds out his plate, with some meat still on it, to*
CORBIN.)

CORBIN: A man should read what he wants. You like
it, you read it. Let's just talk. I prefer to talk. Use my
mind.

(CORBIN *tries to take the plate but* TICE *holds on to it, and at
the same time extends the book to* CORBIN.)

TICE: But that's just it. Living like we do, working like
we do, we can't study our own mind cause it's broken.
This little book puts the pieces back together.

(TICE *extends the book to* CORBIN *with one hand, and the
plate with the other hand.* CORBIN *again tries to take the
plate but* TICE *pulls it back. Again* TICE *holds out the plate
to* CORBIN, *then the book. It is evident that he is letting*
CORBIN *know that if he wants the plate, he'll have to take the
book as well. Finally* CORBIN *understands and takes the book
and plate from* TICE's *hands.*)

TICE: Some of us change, Corbin. Some of us pretend to change. We've made an agreement and whatever else you are, you'll be one or the other in my house from now on. I don't care which.

CORBIN: Can I use your fork?

(TICE *holds his fork out to* CORBIN. CORBIN *reaches for it, but* TICE *snatches it back.* TICE *holds it out again. This* CORBIN *snatches the fork so fast that* TICE *is surprised.*)

(*End Scene Seven*)

Scene Eight

(CORBIN *is alone. He takes out his razor. He unfolds the blade and looks at it. He wipes it on his sleeve. He studies the blade again and suddenly slashes the air.*)

CORBIN: Yeah? Think you're smart? (*He places the knife against his own neck.*)

CORBIN: You think you're smart? Idiot. You're gonna pay. Who's gonna pay? You're gonna pay.

(CALI *enters carrying a bowl of hot water.* CORBIN *quickly quits and sits.*)

CALI: Talkin' to yourself's the second sign of madness, sir.

CORBIN: What's the first? I may be doubly mad. And I should know the worst if I am.

(CALI *puts the bowl in front of* CORBIN.)

CALI: First sign is a white man hidin' out in this house.

(CORBIN *again takes up the razor.*)

CORBIN: That's it then. I guess I'm twice mad. How 'bout you?

CALI: Water won't stay hot just to suit you.

(CORBIN *leans over the bowl and looks at his reflection*)

CORBIN: I don't know. It might. Looks awfully friendly to me. Handsome even.

(CALI *takes a small mirror from her dress pocket and hands it to Corbin.*)

CALI: Before you drown.

(CORBIN *now admires himself in the mirror, one eye on* CALI *through the mirror. She just stands at a distance, not looking at him.*)

CORBIN: Now, how do you see this face? Honest? Prettier than most?

CALI: Is the choice between honest but ugly or pretty but dishonest?

CORBIN: I never been called pretty but a fair few girls have been attached to this face, no two ways about it.

(*Now* CALI *looks at* CORBIN.)

CALI: How few?

CORBIN: I've had more than my fair share. There. Scratch fair few, since you're gonna take issue with that, and replace it with fair share.

CALI: Men who boast about how they've had their fair share most likely been puttin' all their energy into... studyin' themselves, if you know what I mean. (*Beat*) Sir.

(CORBIN *begins to lather up his face.*)

CORBIN: You could do a fellow's confidence permanent damage. Just tryin' to talk myself up since you don't seem to want nothin' to do with me. Can't see why. I know I could do with a bath.

CALI: If you talk this much over a bowl of water I'd hate to see what you'd do before gettin' in a bath.

CORBIN: You might not hate it.

CALI: What?

CORBIN: What you'd see. Me and a bath we sort of go together. I just—

CALI: There you go again. You ever heard of Narcissus?

CORBIN: Heard it's a quiet town.

(CALI *takes the mirror from* CORBIN *just as he's about to start shaving. She holds it in front of his face.*)

CALI: He's from an old Greek myth. He was in love with himself.

CORBIN: Gotta start lovin' somewhere. Practice makes perfect. I practice on myself regularly.

(CALI *takes the razor and it appears as if she will shave* CORBIN. *After a moment she moves away.*)

CORBIN: And what happened to old Narcissus?

CALI: Narcissus. He lost his face. A goddess, angered by his vanity, swooped down and stole his face as punishment. He wandered for eternity, lookin' for himself.

CORBIN: How's he gonna do that? He hasn't got any eyes.

CALI: Exactly.

CORBIN: Damn. That's hard.

CALI: And I have your face here, in this mirror. I might break it.

CORBIN: Seven years bad luck for you.

CALI: And no face. Forever. For you, sir.

(CORBIN *rises, his face still lathered up.*)

CORBIN: And what if Narciss-whatever, accidentally bumped into this goddess?

CALI: Chances are against it.

CORBIN: Just gotta wander and wander?

CALI: Eternity.

CORBIN: This is a small room.

CALI: Eternity doesn't have a size.

CORBIN: And time is passing while the water's gettin' cold. *(Beat)* Want to know what I like?

CALI: No.

CORBIN: I like when it rains and there're no leaks in the roof and you can hear it come down hard and someone's lying right there next to you.

CALI: Want to know what I like?

CORBIN: Yeah.

CALI: When it storms and I know the roof won't hold but it does hold, and the whack of the storm shakes the walls but my bed's warm and I'm lying in it, and no one is lying right there next to me.

CORBIN: No one is my middle name.

(CORBIN takes some lather from his face with a finger and slowly tries to put it on CALI's face. She stops him by holding up the razor as a warning.)

CALI: It's not the same rain we're talking about, mister. Not the same storm. Touch me—And I'll show you. *(She closes the razor, slaps it in his hand and exits.)*

(End Scene Eight)

Scene Nine

(TICE is teaching CORBIN how to soap box.)

TICE: Sometimes all you have is a snap of time. Just that quick to step up and say what you've got to say. Just a snap. The police come, you've got to blend back

into the streets. Like you're nothing. When Harry
Haywood came to Birmingham, I told him to cut out
that fast walking with your head up in the air or these
crackers'll spot you. You've got to get that slouch in
your walk. Look scared, as if you are about to run.
Now, first the snap, step out and loud: *(Bellows out
a strange, shocking cry)* Hot-toe-mali no! Jesus Christ,
Lord forgive me: 'Don't look! Don't look!' That'll get
their attention. Moment they turn towards you, you
plow on in. You've got to know the mind only seems
like a stone: hard, tight, solid. But really it's a bowl of
water and you can throw anything in it. Some of it will
sink but sometimes some of it will float and when the
day comes and they commence to drowning they'll
grab hold of that flotsam and use it.

CORBIN: Don't see myself in public speaking.

TICE: You've been at me for hours to show you how it's
done.

CORBIN: No. I been asking you who's your best box
man.

TICE: The best box man? That'd be me. Now listen and
learn.

CORBIN: I can't speak to crowds. They scare me.

TICE: Hey. You hear me: no other organization will
have you.

CORBIN: So. Might change my mind. Could go back to
Muscatine and

CORBIN/TICE: Cut buttons.

TICE: No. Buttons are done. Out of fashion. It's the zip,
tie or clip these days.

CORBIN: Could join the Klan...

TICE: They won't have you. You're too poor. In
Birmingham, Klan's a middle class organization. They

wear that fine linen over their heads. Though they might let you wash their sheets.

CORBIN: Could join the N A A C P. More respectable than your party.

TICE: They won't have you either. N A A C P are nice people. Nice people aren't poor people. Besides, they've only got one, two, three, four, five, six dues paying members in all of Birmingham. We've got four hundred and ninety three. Want me to count that out so you'll see the difference?

CORBIN: The party down here, it's just a puppet for the Reds in New York. That's what they say. And the Russians. You jump when the Russians call. Jump. Jump.

TICE: Jump. Well, I guess we do sometimes. Just like the N A A C P jumps when their directives are handed down. Just like any local jumps. But the New York cadre aren't here. Neither is Joe Stalin. Our work is local. Ideas are too.

CORBIN: Why do you want me in the party anyway?

TICE: Because you're crippled up a bit and that attracts sympathy. Poor, that makes you like us. Not too ugly. That attracts trust. No family so if the police kill you, no hearts to break.

(CORBIN *is not impressed.*)

TICE: Facts are, we're a bit low on white boys. You see, we, the dirty reds, are mostly black, but for a few whites, some of which are Klansmen gone red. We're mostly unskilled in the party. But we're a party of black and white. And black and white

CORBIN/TICE: must unite.

CORBIN: Why in the hell?

TICE: Because Jesus Christ says the poor, that's us, are all brothers. And his right hand man, a quick little fellow, boils on his ass, goes by the name of Karl, says those who labor, that's us again, even if we are out of work, to make the wealth are one.

CORBIN: Even when we're at each other's throats?

TICE: That's where the bosses want us to be, face to face, rather than—

CORBIN: *(Bored)* side by side.

TICE: That's right. Now shut up and do what I do.

(TICE lets out a "call" again. CORBIN gives a weak imitation.)

TICE: What've you got stuck in your throat? Open up that hole, like this.

(TICE makes the "call" again. CORBIN imitates him, a little better this time, but not much.)

TICE: think what you're missing is that feeling of being choked by the world. You wake up with it in the morning like a hand 'round your throat. All day long it's squeezing. Your call, it's got to break that grip. Now. Let's try this

(TICE suddenly puts his hands around CORBIN's throat. The two men eye one another. For a moment, there is a sense of danger.)

TICE: Now break my hold. No. With your voice.

(CORBIN tries some feeble choked calls. TICE grips him tighter. Suddenly CORBIN lets out a choke-freeing yodel that breaks TICE's grip.)

TICE: You try that in the outhouse and I promise you everything just leap right out of there! Now, when you've got their attention, main thing is, don't ever repeat yourself. You've got to throw them something different every time, making it up as you go:

(Now TICE *soap boxes, and he is impressive in his preaching.)*

TICE: My brothers and sisters. Are you tired of local social workers swinging belts at your back, while you work for a spoonful of nothing and a cupful of less? You may be jobless, but that's no fair relief. Think of your gruelling, daily struggle in terms of...apples. We, my brethren, we are the apples...on the tree. T C I and work relief want us to shrink up so small we forget we're apples and think we're just the... shrivelled sum of our seeds. "But wait!", you say, "Seeds are for planting, rebirth and hope!" *(Chants)* Let's be seeds! We are seeds!

TICE/CORBIN: *(Chant)* Seeds, Seeds, We are seeds.

TICE: But hold on! Wait a minute. Seeds are nothing without the hard flesh of the apple to keep them warm, to protect them from the icy winds til they're ready to burst forth and make a new apple tree. Brothers and Sisters, we are more than the sum of our seeds. We're the apple, the branch and the whole damn tree as well. We will not be divided into our parts. We will be whole or nothing. Therefore, we jobless...apples got to demand a minimum work relief of ten dollars a week, paid in cash, not scrip, and free car fare, free coal. So we're going down to city hall at dusk and we're going down together, as a...bushel, to get what we need.

CORBIN: *(Plays the part of* TICE'*s imaginary street public)* You'll never get ten dollars.

TICE: *(Turns on him, playing the part)* Ah, the white slave speaks. Just how much are you getting paid now, young man?

CORBIN: I'm not.

TICE: Work relief?

CORBIN: Red Cross wouldn't take any more of us on.

TICE: But are you not a man? Do you not need to eat?

CORBIN: I need to eat, yeah. I am a man.

TICE: Then you are one of us. Come and walk and shout with us. We can get ten dollars. We can get a whole lot more.

CORBIN: A bullet in the back too.

TICE: We get thousands on the street, we'll make those bullets turn tail, shoot right back up their barrels.

CORBIN: You sound like a. Commie. Dirty red, you are! Want to mix the races. Give these stupid people big ideas until their heads go pop. You want to make us believe that we're equal, me and you.

TICE: Nah. I'm not here to teach you to see me as equal, to behold my humanity. You're here to learn why you're so small, soul all squashed up in the back of your neck, your eyes, your big blue eyes, like two assholes holding their breath. Look at yourself. You're nothing but a pit sucking, coal shittin

CORBIN: Crippled up

TICE: road trash piece of bukra

CORBIN: peckerwood

TICE: pork-skinned

CORBIN: son of a pig's bitch

TICE: about to be slaughtered with a fork

CORBIN: because the knife's too good for me.

TICE: See you at dusk for the march.

CORBIN: I'll be there.

TICE: What did I tell you? It works.

(End Scene Nine)

Scene Ten

(CORBIN *is alone with the little book. But the little book is on the floor. He gives it a small kick, then quickly looks around to make sure he is still alone and no one has seen this. He gives the book a slightly stronger kick and the book slides across the floor. Suddenly* TICE *appears from outside. He has been beaten. His shirt is torn and bloody.* CORBIN *just stares at him.)*

TICE: What the hell is my book doing on the floor?

(CORBIN *snatches up the book, dusts it off and hesitantly offers it to* TICE, *who starts to take it but then pulls his hand back.)*

TICE: No. Blood.

CORBIN: What happened—

TICE: *(Interrupts, quietly)* Read to me.

CORBIN: Why don't I—

TICE: *(Harsh)* I said read to me.

(CORBIN *is unsettled by this and opens the book at random)*

CORBIN: "Differences of...age and sex have no longer any distinctive social...validity for the working class. All are instruments of labour, more or less expensive to use, according to their age and sex..."

TICE: When I rewrite that book, it'll say "more or less expensive to use, according to their age and sex and race." 'Cause here in Alabama, we are the center of the party, colored women and men, our focus is on our lives and works. Not yours, not yours Corbin Teel. We're the core. Got to be that way or nothing will change. Read.

CORBIN: "It has been objected that upon the abolition of private property all work will cease, and universal laziness will overtake us."

TICE: *(Finishing it for him, though in pain).* "According to this, bourgeois society ought long ago to have gone to the dogs through sheer idleness;

CORBIN: For those of its members who work, acquire nothing, and those who acquire anything

TICE/CORBIN: do not work."

TICE: No. No. I read those pieces to you yesterday. You read me something else.

CORBIN: I don't want to read.

TICE: Why?

CORBIN: What happened to you?

TICE: I said why?

CORBIN: I'll get some water.

TICE: Read the book.

CORBIN: No.

TICE: Say it, Corbin. Say it now or I'll start screamin out the door I've got a murderer in my house and they'll come and finish us both off.

CORBIN: You don't know if that foreman died.

TICE: I know.

CORBIN: I didn't mean to kill him.

TICE: How stupid do you think I am? That I didn't know the moment I laid eyes on you, heard your talk, listened to that tick, tick, tick? You're no surprise to me.

CORBIN: You're saying I'm a cold blooded killer? That what you're saying?!

TICE: No! I'm saying you can't read! *(Beat)* Knew it the first time you opened the book. Asking me to read it first so you could hear how it sounded. Line after line. And then you'd memorise. And I'll be damned if you didn't memorise 'bout half that book. You're good. Oh, you're good. What're you after? Most men like you, they can't read. Aren't ashamed of it, neither. Why're you so good at pretending you're just a little like me?

CORBIN: There's blood on your mouth.

TICE: I said what are you after, Corbin Teel?

(Blood has trickled down TICE's chin. CORBIN crosses the stage to TICE, hesitantly. Then CORBIN uses his fingers to wipe the blood gently from TICE's mouth. Then some moments of silence as the men look at one another.)

CORBIN: Let me have a look.

(TICE reluctantly let's CORBIN open his shirt. CORBIN touches TICE's ribs and TICE stifles his pain.)

CORBIN: Maybe some ribs cracked.

TICE: Where's Cali?

(TICE moves away , his back to CORBIN. CORBIN slowly begins to unbutton his own shirt. CORBIN twists his shirt into a rope, and approaches TICE from behind. Only at the last moment to we realize it's to bind TICE's ribs.)

CORBIN: Deliverin' sheets. "Going over the Mountain," she said. We'll to have to wrap you up. Tight. So those ribs can heal. Not as bad as it looks. Mostly just blood.

TICE: I could teach you to read. But you've got to ask.

CORBIN: Nah. Too late.

TICE: Half the party can't read. They pair us up. One's that can read've got to teach the ones that can't. And when they begin to read, they begin to figure.

(CORBIN has finished binding)

CORBIN: Tell me what happened. You get in a fight at the pool hall? You mangy old rascal you.

(TICE is silent. Then he starts to laugh, even though it hurts him. CORBIN laughs too.)

TICE: Fifth time we'd moved the meeting since June.
Don't know how they found out where we were. Been
working on a postcard campaign to the mayor for
protection from eviction. Building up to a big march
on city hall next month, make the mayor hear us out.
(Beat) They had him on the floor and two of them stood
on his hands. A man on each hand while a third one
started to count. One, two, three, four. He broke the
fingers on each hand. Of your man, Clyde Johnson,
the one you never met. I was in the corner, thinking
what a lucky bastard he was. Just his fingers. Not that
they won't kill a white man. Tenant farmer J W Davis
lynched for working with the Sharecroppers Union.
But more likely it's just fingers. Ralph Grey. They
didn't break his fingers. He was a colored man so they
shot him instead. And not just once. Back, chest. Back,
chest. Dumped his body on the steps of the courthouse.
In a crowd there, kicking and shooting his body,
though he was long dead.

CORBIN: Problem with the Klan *(Beat)* you can't see
their faces.

TICE: Wasn't the Klan. It was the Police, T C I guards,
and any white man on the street who wanted to take
part. Men of good standing. Men who wear the buttons
you made in Muscatine. Men who go home to good
pies and meats for dinner, touch their women late in
the night. *(Beat)* Then they went through the streets.
Word is dozens wounded and dead.

CORBIN: You're safe now.

TICE: You are too. All this mess and they've forgotten
about your foreman.

CORBIN: Maybe.

TICE: If you really did kill a foreman. If you name is
Corbin Teel.

CORBIN: You're gonna be pretty sore tomorrow.

TICE: In a couple days. When this cools down. I want you to get out.

CORBIN: I like you. I'll go by your rules. But both of us know that all I got to do is open that door and then what you got over me in here, Mister Hogan, is the same as nothing out there. So I'll stay here long as I want. Meanwhile. *(Beat)* You teach me to read. I've got to learn how to impress.

TICE: Impress all you like. You touch her and I'll

TICE/CORBIN: Kill you.

CORBIN: How could we look at this in terms of apples?

TICE: I'm gonna crush you up into cider with my own bare hands.

CORBIN: I won't harm your daughter.

TICE: And suck up the juice.

CORBIN: You have my word.

TICE: Yeah, I have your word and you can't even read it.

(Suddenly CORBIN is at TICE's side. He holds the book open between them, so they can both read it.)

CORBIN: So teach me. One word at a time. Then I'll read it back to you. *(Beat)* Read the god damn book!

(TICE doesn't look down at the book but instead says the words from memory, looking elsewhere. CORBIN looks at the page.)

TICE: First thing I did to learn myself is I counted out the letters. Then the words. Something about knowing what it was all made up of, helped me—

CORBIN: *(Interrupts)* Just show me.

TICE: A.

CORBIN: A.

TICE: Spectre.

CORBIN: Spectre.

TICE: is.

CORBIN: is.

TICE: haunting.

CORBIN: haunting.

TICE: That's eight letters.

CORBIN: Okay. Now say the letters for me. *(Beat)* Say the letters.

(TICE is silent some moments.)

TICE: U.

CORBIN: U.

TICE: R.

CORBIN: R.

TICE: A.

CORBIN: A.

TICE: Son-of-a-bitch.

(CORBIN just looks at TICE. TICE will not look at him, just stares elsewhere.)

CORBIN: Let's read a different page. Always something better on the other side, right?

TICE: Party can't use a man like you. You've got no-

CORBIN: What.

TICE: Foundation. *(Beat)* That's F O U N.

CORBIN: Turn the page. You will teach me to read. And that way I'll know everything that you know

(CORBIN *holds the book out in front of himself, the pages open and facing* TICE. *The men stand in silence, facing one another. Black out)*

END ACT ONE

ACT TWO

Prelude

(Without warning, TICE *suddenly appears in the public, sharpening a small piece of steel, a home-made blade. The stone against the steel makes an eerie sound that echoes from another world. We hear this sounds a few times as he speaks. Tice is wearing the the same clothes as in* ACT ONE, *but a different shirt.)*

TICE: You ever had a knife at your throat? It's overrated. A knife at my throat I can see doesn't bother me the way the ones I can't see, do. 'Cause most of us have got the ones we can't see circling 'round our neck and all your life you've got to watch which way you turn your head or you'll get. Stuck. *(He holds out the knife.)* Here, how sharp it is? Feel it. See how it shines? *(Now he withdraws the real knife and slowly holds out his other hand with the invisible knife in it.)* And this one, the one you can't see, feel that blade. Go on. Touch it. Just touch it. *(Beat)* There's nothing like it. *(Suddenly he throws the invisible knife high up into the air above him. He does some wild dodges and then catches the invisible knife in the air, perfectly.)* Damn I like that one. One of my soap box favourites: the invisible knife. And this takes me back to...apples. Over the years, it started to rub on me, how I used the apple. The fruits of labor, the apple tree family. Etceteras. But then I got to thinkin' 'bout the apple and yeah, its flesh is white, with all these little black seeds inside and I thought hmmm. Follow it a little further and the good part, the sweet part is the white flesh. Who cares about those little black seeds? You eat one by mistake, you just *(does three quick spits)*. Not a second thought. So I quit on the apples. Gave them a rest for a while. But it creeps up on me, because the seeds are, naturally, at the core; the seed is the core. You swallow one, it shoots right back out, ready to make a tree wherever it lands. *(Says the following in one, smooth breath:)* And then it comes to me a little further that maybe an apple is just an apple for a horse not a man and better left out of conversation all together.

Things fall apart, yeah. They do. With time. But what's the reason and what's the rhyme?

(TICE lightly, purposely, touches one of the sheets piled on the floor. As he exits, the sheet begins to glow, then rise.)

(End Prologue)

Scene One

(In the dark, CALI is asleep on a large pile of sheets on the floor. These sheets seem to glow in the darkness with a strange, ethereal light. Magically, a sheet rises from it's pile and floats in the air above her. If possible, more than one sheet rises up, perhaps two or three. The sheets float around the stage like ghosts. After some moments, she sits up in her "dream", and marvels at the floating sheets. She reaches to grab one, but it evades her. She tries again.)

CALI: Come back here, you.

(CALI follows the sheet/sheets around the room, mesmerized by it, jumping for it, laughing as it evades her, enjoying the strange game.)

CALI: Now stay put. Hey! Stop that! Come back down. Damn. Way up there. Give me a ride. Won't you give me a ride?

(Finally CALI *gives up and sits back down on the pile of sheets. When she does so, the sheet, or sheets, floats down into her arms, and she "wakes" and begins to sing as she gathers the sheets.)*

CALI: *(Sings)* Church offers me a sermon sweet
bar begs me to move my feet
meetin' discusses how we all gonna eat
but only place I'm gonna be
is both ends of a whiteman's sheet
both ends of a whiteman's sheet
Shee-eet, Shee-eet, Shee-eet.

*(*CORBIN *enters the room, with a bowl of porridge. He repeats the last line of* CALI's *song.)*

CORBIN: *(Sings)* Both ends of a whiteman's sheet.

CALI: *(Coldly)* What do you think would happen in Shades Valley and Mountain Brooks if their sheets never came back to their house?

CORBIN: Guess they'd sleep in their towels.

CALI: I'm washing those too.

CORBIN: Well, then they'd wrap up in their curtains.

CALI: They're out back with the shirts.

CORBIN: You know, there's other things you can do with sheets besides fold them. May I, Ma'am?

*(*CORBIN *takes the other end of the sheet and carefully wraps her in it.)*

CORBIN: You can wear it like a. Greek Goddess.

CALI: Nah. Too tight. And those Goddesses were always fightin' over babies and fruit. Not my style. Eat your porridge or it'll get cold. *(She twirls herself from the sheet.)*

CORBIN: You could make a tent. *(He gets under the sheet and spreads his arms to make a kind of tent.)* Hey, pretty

Lady, would you like to come in and see my tent?
(He dances around her as a "tent", but she shakes her head "no".)

CALI: Besides, looks like the Klan. I don't like it.

(CORBIN drops his arms and speaks as a ghost under the sheets.)

CORBIN: I'm not the Klan. I'm a good citizen.

CALI: There's a difference?

(CORBIN pulls the sheet off and stares at CALI.)

CORBIN: Tell me what I need to do to get close to you.

CALI: Keep your distance. That way you'll get close enough. Meanwhile, why don't you take hold of some of these and help me fold 'em.

(CALI gives CORBIN the end of a sheet and they straighten and fold it together.)

CORBIN: Look. I understand why its a. Difficult thing for you and me.

CALI: Hold the corners so I can pull 'em tight.

CORBIN: Another man. He'd take what he wanted. No one to stop him.

(CALI stops folding for a moment.)

CORBIN: But I'm not like other. Men. I am. Decent. Yeah, a decent man.

(CALI doesn't respond.)

CORBIN: Tell me what I have to do.

CALI: Just stand still. Don't move.

CORBIN: That's all? Hey. What are you doing?

(Now CALI is wrapping CORBIN in a sheet. She does this easily and expertly so that before he knows what is happening, he's wearing the sheet)

CORBIN: I can't move my arms. *(He is wrapped in the sheet, which looks like a makeshift dress.)* Cali, girl. What is your game?

CALI: Ask me how you look.

CORBIN: How do I look?

CALI: You look like a girl.

CORBIN: Am I pretty?

CALI: No. But I can take care of that.

CORBIN: Go on then.

(CALI takes shoe polish from her dress. She puts it on CORBIN's face.)

CORBIN: Hey. Stop that!

CALI: Quiet, Corbin Teel. You want me to play with you, you do it my way. *(She continues applying the shoe polish as he speaks.)*

CORBIN: Well, I admit I kinda had something else in mind... If your father comes home and sees me like this...

CALI: Shhh!

(CORBIN relents and CALI finishes his face, which is now black with shoe polish. She fluffs his hair, stands back to look.)

CORBIN: Now you gonna kiss this girl or what?

(CALI just looks at CORBIN.)

CORBIN: Hey. I didn't let you dress me up for nothing. Come here. Kiss me.

CALI: Give me your shoe.

CORBIN: Huh?

CALI: I need your shoe.

CORBIN: Okay... Yeah...alright. Lets start taking things off.

(CORBIN *kicks off one of his shoes.* CALI *picks it up and puts it on her hand as a puppet.*)

CALI: Now, repeat after me: "Oh, please don't, sir."

(CORBIN *uncertainly shakes his head "no".*)

CALI: It's a sweet game. I promise. Now repeat after me or we won't play: "Oh, please don't, sir!"

CORBIN: *(Dead pan)* "Oh, please don't, sir."

CALI: "I have to hurry!"

CORBIN: *(Dead pan)* "I have to hurry."

CALI: "Scurry!"

CORBIN: *(Less dead pan)* "Scurry!"

CALI: "Worry!"

CORBIN: *(Now copies her intonation)* "Worry!"

CALI: "No offence but please just don't!"

CORBIN: *(Playing it up)* "Just please, please don't!"

(CALI *and* CORBIN *watch each other for a moment, then she throws down the shoe and picks up a handful of porridge. She smears it on her face until she's wearing a white mask of porridge. He watches her, disturbed.*)

CALI: There. How's that. How do I look?

CORBIN: I don't think I'm liking this game.

CALI: What's the matter, little girl doesn't want to play? Little girl wants a kiss, does she?

(CALI *makes kissing noises as she approaches* CORBIN. *He steps back, almost involuntarily.*)

CALI: Oh. Little girl wants more than a kiss? *(She circles him, talking sweetly)* Problem with you, little girl. Little. Savage. Girl. You want it all. *(Beat)* I see the lust in your eyes, bitch. I smell the sex on your breath. You're just waiting for me to take it, aren't you? *(She lightly brushes her hand across his groin. She tuts her disapproval.)* You ought to be ashamed. Wet as you are. I could turn you inside out.

(Now CORBIN *violently frees himself from the sheet. He pins* CALI *to the floor and kneels over her. He unbuckles his belt. It seems he is ready to force her. She strikes him in the face. He freezes.)*

CALI: Corbin Teel. Now I see you. All these days I wasn't sure but now I see you clear: a decent man.

*(*CORBIN *stares at* CALI *for some moments. Then he moves away from her, stunned by what he was about to do.)*

CORBIN: Jesus, Cali.

(After some moments, CORBIN *wipes his face on one of the sheets.* CALI *grabs the sheet from him.)*

CALI: Don't you ruin my sheets. Sit down.

*(*CORBIN *sits.)*

CORBIN: I'm sorry.

*(*CALI *spits on a rag and tosses it to him to wipe his face.)*

CORBIN: Please, Cali. I'm sorry.

(After some moments:)

CALI: There are parts of me you cannot know. You want something? Here. *(She scrapes some porridge from her face.)* You can have this. *(She roughly smears it across his mouth.)* But I tell you one thing, Corbin Teel. You will not dream on my body.

*(*CALI *leaves the room.* CORBIN *looks after her. After she is gone, he slowly wipes his mouth. Then he cleans the polish from his face.)*

(End Scene One)

Scene Two

(TICE, *and* CORBIN *are finishing dinner.* TICE *is reading outloud* . CORBIN *picks at the calloses on his hands with his razor.*)

TICE: "But not only has the bourgeoisie"—

(CORBIN *makes a long, strange, irritating noise.* TICE *stops.* TICE *starts reading again, patiently.*)

TICE: "But not only has the bourgeoisie"—

(CORBIN *again makes a long, ugly noise*)

TICE: In my house, Mister Teel, you will listen to me read. Or no more soup.

CORBIN: In your house, I can get my own soup now.

(TICE *just stares at him a moment, then continues.*)

TICE: "But not only has the bourgeoisie forged the weapons that bring death to itself; it has also called into existence the men who are to wield those weapons—"

CORBIN: Are we done for tonight? Seems like we're just turnin' somersaults here. Why won't you quit this readin' and take me to a meeting with you? Let me meet the rest of the men.

TICE: But some men do not fight for their brethren.

CORBIN: I could follow you one night, you know. I could follow you and bring the roof down.

(TICE *finds another section and reads.*)

TICE: But some men, they become "an appendage of the machine." (*He stares at* CORBIN.)

CORBIN: Don't look at me. Shit. I'm not the one sounding like some machine. Tell me something. This Karl the-plug-ugly-beard-man-Marx. He wrote that bitty book of yours. And he's white.

TICE: Jewish.

CORBIN: Skin's white. Just like me. And he's dead. And
you've got his words all stuffed up in your mouth. Live
by 'em. It don't figure.

TICE: I don't live by them. I use them.

CORBIN: You eat his words.

TICE: Yeah. And I mix them with Du Bois, Garvey, the
Bible. Lots of things. All good words of justice they
come from. Some kind of heaven. Maybe that's right.
But what's driving those words comes from the motor
right here under our feet, what we learned fighting a
slave-owning culture with something you could never
imagine: spectacular resistance and spirit-

CORBIN: *(Interrupts)* Nah, nah, nah. All you seem to
know how to do is talk, Tice. Tice-the-talker. Yeah.

(CALI enters.)

CORBIN: It's a pretty way to move in the world but
some of us, our bodies get in the way and we can't find
the talk for it. Like this. *(He takes out his razor and cuts
his own arm.)* I think a man's natural state is to bleed,
not to talk. What do you think, Cali?

(CALI just watches CORBIN.)

TICE: You've got it backwards. We talk so we don't
have to bleed. I think I'll have another potato. Pass the
salt, comrade.

(CORBIN doesn't respond.)

CALI: Oh, today he's a comrade. Yesterday he was an
S O B.

TICE: Do you mock me in front of guests?

CALI: Now he's also a guest.

CORBIN: Actually I'm a po-ten-tial member of the Party.
The key word here being

TICE/CORBIN: Potential.

CORBIN: And there's no end of potential in this room. Cali, let me help you with the dishes.

TICE: You will not help her with the dishes. Your po-ten-tial shrivels with your even thinking about it. Now pass the salt.

(CORBIN *calculatingly knocks the salt to the floor.*)

CORBIN: Get your own salt. Damn. Spilled salt. Means the devil's gonna get your ass, Tice. Can the party protect you from the devil?

(TICE *retrieves the salt.*)

TICE: We're in session over that right now. But that's my problem. You're problem is you are not, after all, what you think you are.

CALI: Get on your marks.

CORBIN: And what does that mean?

CALI: Get set.

TICE: Let me explain.

CORBIN: You better do that.

CALI: Go.

TICE: But you'll have to close your eyes. You have to listen, not look. It's your lookin' that's got you where you are now. It's your seein that's twisted your mind. Twisted your soul into believin' that the pursuit of property, which is kin to the pursuit and consolidation of whiteness—

CALI: This is going to be good.

TICE: —really might be the pursuit of happiness. *(Beat)* Got it?

CORBIN: This's got somethin' to do with salt?

(CALI *giggles.*)

TICE: *(To* CALI*)* Damn it, you won't learn from me so let him do it.

CALI: I just don't like to see you waste your time, Daddy.

CORBIN: Now wait just a darn minute—

TICE: *(To* CORBIN*)* But Cali's right. Until you've proven otherwise, you're neither a comrade nor a guest. Nor are you...

CORBIN: What? An idiot? *(To* CALI*)* Now you heard it from your father first: Cali, I am not an idiot.

TICE: No. You're not an idiot, but neither are you a white man.

CORBIN: Huh?

TICE: Your heard me.

CORBIN: No. Don't think I did. Say it again.

TICE: No.

CORBIN: Say it again.

CALI: He said.

TICE: Don't you speak for me.

CALI: He said.

TICE: I said: You. Are. Not. A. White. Man. There. Don't make me say it again.

CORBIN: Damn.

TICE: It's a hard truth. Hard and ugly and I don't like saying it but some things have got to be said.

CALI: And all this time I thought.

TICE: What?

CALI: I was sure he was-

TICE: *(To* CORBIN*)* There have always been black and white, right? But that's a lie. There were slaves in

Greece and Rome, long ago, but they knew nothing
about race.

CALI: Imagine. A better world. Too bad it's behind us.

TICE: They made their divisions between civilised and
barbarian. And you could have a white skin and be a
slave.

CALI: Sounds like my kind of heaven.

TICE: A black skin and be civilised.

CALI: Well I'll be damned. I'm going to die right here at
this table—

TICE: Oppression was justified in terms of culture, not
race.

CALI: —and be born again a Roman.

TICE: *(To* CALI*)* Cali. I may not inspire in you a feeling
for books, but please shut up and let him learn.

CALI: Alright. I'll go and wash your socks, Father.

TICE: Good. *(To* CORBIN*)* You became a white man only
'cause I was said to be colored.

CALI: I can smell them stinkin' from the other room.
(She doesn't move.)

CORBIN: Then if I'm not white, you're not colored.

TICE: Not until the slave trade gave me that definition.

CALI: Finished all the sheets from that big white house.

TICE: What I'm saying is white is not how you're born,
it's what you're paid.

CALI: Now I can start on your laundry. Both of yours.

TICE: Your wages are the privileges that come with
acting white.

CORBIN: I don't. Act white. I'm just. Me.

TICE: No. No. You are a white "me". A white Corbin Teel. And you have a ticket in your pocket which is now sewn to your ass. And that ticket says you get privileges. If not money, then laws that'll decide in your favour.

CORBIN: You got a ticket?

TICE: Well. Well then. Yes, I have.

CALI: Let me guess. Your ticket, unlike Corbin's, says you're getting on the train at the back of the station. No peanuts served. When the tracks break down, lay down in front of the train and help it pass over.

TICE: Exactly.

(CALI suddenly throws a cup of water in CORBIN's face. CORBIN and TICE are stunned.)

CALI: How dare you come into this house masquerading as a white man. Give me that damn ticket, I'm gonna tear it to pieces.

TICE: Won't make no odds. He'll just run on back to Daddy and get him another one.

CORBIN: Hey, listen up. The both of you: I've got no ticket. I've got nothin' but the shirt on my back. That enough to make me white?

TICE: A shirt is property.

CORBIN: But this is your god damn shirt!

TICE: That's not the point.

CORBIN: You lent it to me after I bloodied mine up to bind your busted ribs.

TICE: Nevertheless, if you take it and sell it you'll get a better price for it than I could because

CORBIN: of my ticket. Bullshit. It's just a shirt.

CALI: Actually, it's my shirt. My father gave it to me last winter. Too small for him.

(CORBIN *smells the shirt.*)

CORBIN: *(To* CALI*)* I'm wearing your shirt?

CALI: It's yours now.

TICE: And property is privilege.

CALI: You're right, Daddy. Every little bit counts.

CORBIN: So this is all about having clothes?

TICE: No. It's a way of seeing things.

CORBIN: Well. Then I guess there's only one way to find out. I'll take off my clothes. Right here where I stand. And then we'll see what we've got.

TICE: I don't think my daughter would take too kindly to that in her house.

CALI: Father, let him do what he dares.

(CALI *and* TICE *look at one another.* CORBIN *looks back and forth at both of them, not sure if it's a game.*)

CORBIN: *(Challenging)* All right. Shit. Yeah. Okay. *(He takes off his shoes one by one, undressing methodically. Then, he dramatically takes off his shirt. He is now, partly, undressing for* CALI.*)* How'm I doin'?

CALI: Some of that shine is comin' off your...face.

CORBIN: You like it?

(CALI *gives him a first real smile.* CORBIN *laughs in triumph, standing only in his long pants, and makes to get dressed again. He puts his shirt half way on.*)

TICE: Finish what you started, Corbin Teel. Go on.

CALI: Daddy!

TICE: A man that doesn't finish what he's started is only half a man. Cali doesn't like things by half. Neither do I. And neither does the communist party.

(CORBIN *considers this, then begins to unbutton his pants.* CALI *turns away and stays turned away.*)

CALI: Don't. You've gone far enough.

(CORBIN *stops. He looks at* TICE.)

TICE: Go on.

CORBIN: What kind of game we playin' at?

TICE: Not a game. A test.

CORBIN: What for?

TICE: Just want to see what lengths you'll go to make yourself a new man.

(*After a moment,* CORBIN *takes off his pants.*)

TICE: Finish up.

(CORBIN *hesitates a long moment, then takes off his underwear. He just stand there, naked.*)

TICE: Well, well. What have we got here now?

CORBIN: *(Quietly)* A man with nothing. If I knew how, I'd spell it out to you. Lowest man on earth.

TICE: That's right.

CORBIN: No more no fuckin' less.

TICE: Hmmm. I'd say you're a little more than less. And look at the battle scar on that leg.

CORBIN: Yeah. A hole right down to the bone. Maybe that's where I lost all my property.

(TICE *jumps up as though he's had a revelation.*)

TICE: Wait a minute. Just wait a damn minute. There's nothing changed here. You're not a naked man, but an idiot to take off your clothes, degrade yourself and insult a woman that I do declare was actually beginning to like you.

CORBIN: Cali?

TICE: *(To* CALI*)* Leave the room, daughter.

(CALI *walks a few steps away and stops.*)

CORBIN: Cali. Please.

TICE: You're looking sort of goose pimply too. Are you cold?

CORBIN: *(To* CALI'*s back)* I took the ticket. Like you take a drink of water. Yeah. I didn't know what it all meant but I knew it would clear a path to walk on. And it would give me some little bit of hope that I wouldn't be last. That someone else would do that for me. *(Beat)* Can you want me, as I am?

TICE: Blow me down, not sentiment.

CORBIN: Could you want me as I wasn't made to be?

(CALI *does not turn around, but she is listening.)*

CORBIN: I'll stop being what I am. Your father says it's possible.

CALI: In here, not out there.

CORBIN: *(Quietly)* Touch me. Cali. Please. Touch me.

(CALI *stands silently, then she leaves the room.* CORBIN *and* TICE *are silent a moment.)*

CORBIN: Whatever I am. *(Beat)* I am a man.

TICE: Yeah. That you are. *(Beat)* And I'm an apple seed.

(CORBIN *now moves to gather his clothes.)*

TICE: Tomorrow. You get out.

(End Scene Two)

Scene Three

(CORBIN *is alone. Polishing his shoes with the sleeve of his shirt.* CALI *enters. She just stands there and watches him.)*

CORBIN: Just trying to put some shine back in my shoes. You sorry about me leavin'?

CALI: More room in this room after you're gone. No.

CORBIN: I don't believe you.

CALI: Suit yourself.

CORBIN: Hey. You don't say "sir" anymore. Like you used to. But I like it that you don't use it too. It makes us more familiar. *(Beat)* I think you are. Delightful.

CALI: Delightful. A fancy word.

CORBIN: I'm gettin fancier by the minute. I can spell my name out now. And this morning your father learned me that in the 1930 election campaign, the communist party endorsed a black candidate for governor: Walter Lewis. No political party's done that since reconstruc—

CALI: *(Interrupts)* Corbin Teel. Don't even think 'bout giving me history. But here's another little piece for you my own Daddy likes to forget. 1929. John Owens, in the national. He was dead set against bringing colored folks into the communist party 'cause—and for your benefit I'll quote— *(She imitates John Owen's voice:)* "The vast majority of Southern Negroes are not revolutionary, not even radical. Given a society of peace, prosperity and security, they are content to drift through life."

CORBIN: Oh.

CALI: You ever met anyone who was content to drift through life? I have not.

CORBIN: Owens. Huh. Sounds like a man still using his ticket.

CALI: And how do you 'sound' like a man?

(CORBIN considers this, then makes a series of strange, loud, "new" noises. CALI bursts out laughing.)

CORBIN: A new kind of creature. That's all me. *(Beat)* When you laugh. *(He hesitates.)*

CALI: Don't.

CORBIN: All right.

(They are silent.)

CALI: Oh, go on then.

CORBIN: When you laugh. I hear. Haydn.

CALI: Haydn. When did you ever hear Haydn?

CORBIN: Never did. But your father says there's this Ted Wellman. Russian Jew. Known for his. Marxian interpretation. Of a Haydn symphony. *(Beat)* I figure it must be. Interesting music.

CALI: Interesting.

CORBIN: And beautiful to the ear.

CALI: Rather have something from your mouth than Haydn.

CORBIN: You think your father's wrong?

CALI: I think children play. Just as we do.

CORBIN: Then maybe it's time you left your Daddy's house. You're not his wife.

CALI: No, I'm not. But watch your step, Mr. Teel. I am my father's friend. And he is mine. That kind of thing, you don't know.

CORBIN: Cali Hogan. I could stand here and look at you all my life. *(Beat)* Kiss me.

CALI: No.

CORBIN: I'm leaving tomorrow. Just give me one little real-small-tiny-happens-so-fast-you-hardly-notice-what-the-hell-was-that kiss.

CALI: A kiss won't teach you to read.

CORBIN: I bet you haven't kissed a man since your husband got sick and died.

CALI: Better you get back to your books. You don't have much time left.

CORBIN: But a kiss falls under the same. Category. As a book.

CALI: Really.

CORBIN: And is the best. Instrument. For teaching a cracker 'bout. Dialectical materialism.

CALI: Dialectical materialism.

CORBIN: Yes. *(As he speaks the following, he does so as if remembering a lesson, but adding his own as he goes.)* The way I've come to learn it from your father is everythin' is. Material. At this moment, now, that's our mouths too. And change happens through the. Struggle of opposites. That being your mouth and my mouth. Locked in struggle. Cause everythin' is made up of different. Elements. That are in opposition. So, conflict of opposing forces. Leads to growth, change and development. *(Beat)* You need to kiss me so that I can have my development.

CALI: I think Marx was talking about class, not kiss.

CORBIN: I'm dyin' here, Cali. Dyin' of a. Dialectical disadvantage. I've got no way to really comprehend how it all works.

CALI: And my mouth is. Your book.

CORBIN: That's a fact. *(He speaks as though quoting)* But I'm not there yet. And I've got to make it there so I can be right here. 'Cause half way lost is worse than being gone. *(Beat)* Made that bit up myself. You like it?

CALI: I like it better this time with your clothes on. Now you get yourself ready to go.

CORBIN: Anything could happen out there. I don't want to leave. You could make me stay.

CALI: No.

(CALI moves to leave. CORBIN's voice stops her.)

CORBIN: Sleepin on this floor, night after night. Sound of your father turnin' those pages. Like a lullaby. No. Like something else. I don't know. And then there was you, just there in the next room. Even when I was asleep I was more awake than I'd ever been.

(CALI *approaches him.*)

CALI: Don't move. You move and I stop.

(CORBIN *nods.* CALI *unbuttons his shirt. He watches her hands. Then she puts her hands inside his shirt and begins to touch his chest. He closes his eyes, letting her touch him, drinking it in.*)

CORBIN: Don't.

(CALI *takes her hands away.*)

CORBIN: You're only touchin' me cause I'm leaving. Candy for the trash on its way out?

(CALI *slaps* CORBIN.)

CALI: Don't you mock me.

CORBIN: Then why?

CALI: I don't know. Maybe because I forgot. I forgot for a whole minute and it felt so damn good.

CORBIN: Touch me again.

CALI: Can't. Cause now I remember.

CORBIN: Then let me touch you.

CALI: No. (*Beat*) But you can watch me. Touching.

(CALI *slowly, sensuously puts her hand on different places on her body as she speaks, and not necessarily sexual places, but also on her ribs, her breast-bone, her arm, neck.*)

CALI: Here is where I cut myself as a child. Here, where I burned when the fields caught fire. Here is where my mother touched me. I can't remember, but I know it's her. This is where I stripped the corn. This is where

I slept too long. And this place, here, you can never know.

CORBIN: Cali.

(CALI *puts her hand on her forehead.*)

CALI: And this is where you knocked on the door.

(CALI *and* CORBIN *just look at each other. Then she looks away. He is unsettled by desire and uncertainty.*)

CORBIN: Shit. Please, Cali. I never met a woman like you. Hard nosed. Arrogant. Persistent. Just like your father. A fucking communist through and through. *(Beat)* That's a compliment.

(CORBIN *steps a little closer.* CALI'*s voice stops him.*)

CALI: There's nothing here for you, with me.

CORBIN: Yeah, there is. Look at me.

(CALI *looks away*)

CALI: I don't need to look at you to see you, Corbin Teel. One thing I never liked 'bout white men: there's no tomorrow in their face.

CORBIN: Take another look. Maybe you can find something there.

(CALI *now looks at* CORBIN, *then he slowly moves to kiss her. As he does so, she raises her hand to cover his mouth, so her palm will catch his kiss. He hesitates only slightly and then kisses the palm of her hand, as though it were her mouth. The two of them are not touching each other, except to kiss eachother through her hand. They hold the kiss a long moment. Then they quit, and he moves away from her, no longer looking at her. They stand in silence some moments.*)

CORBIN: I think if they didn't go back to those houses, the sheets you wash? I think those folks'd use their damn cash to sleep on, tell themselves as they always have that it's a gift from God sent to keep them warm. *(Beat)* Me, I been cold all my life.

(End Scene Three)

Scene Four

(A small chopping block rolls into the room, from another direction than in scene one. Then a very small log rolls in after it. TICE follows, proudly carrying the ax. He lines up the small log and gets ready to swing. He hesitates. The alignment isn't quite right. He adjusts it again. He swings back with the ax. Just then CALI enters.)

CALI: There's my ax.

TICE: Yes. Yes. Here's your ax and it's Friday today and I'm going to split the logs for the fire.

(CALI stares at the little log.)

CALI: Log. More like a piece of straw.

TICE: Never underestimate the power of the little ones. *(Beat)* He's out back.

CALI: What if someone—

TICE: No one'll see him. I've hung your sheets in a circle.

CALI: What for?

TICE: He's having a bath. I gave him some of that soap you use.

CALI: That soap belongs to the Graftons! For their sheets only.

TICE: He begged me for a bath. Can't have him leave this house all stinked up and yellow.

(After some moments:)

CALI: Daddy, he wants me.

TICE: Yeah. He wants you, Cali. But there's no meanin' to it.

CALI: You like him. I never seen you work so hard to teach a man to read. He's under your skin. And he's under mine too.

TICE: That's what he wants. What he's working for. So stay out of his way.

CALI: He'll never get to a meetin'.

TICE: No, he may never get to a meeting but I tell you he's going out of this house a changed man. He had no eagerness when he came in. Spirit all flickering dull in the back of his skull, 'bout to go out.

CALI: Yeah. And a meanness in his eyes, like small change.

TICE: That's right. And all these days, I've been stoking that little flame. Yeah, I've been bringing it back to life. But a flame like that is hungry. Not just for learning but for flesh so I told him there's women in the Party, some very fine, revolutionary comrades outside this house.

CALI: Yeah...Helen Longs, Estelle Milner *(Mocks)* Cornelia Foreman.

TICE: Alice Mosely. Addie Adkins. Eula Gray.

CALI: No.

TICE: You're the same as them, Cali. It's where you belong. You just don't know it.

CALI: Its not just your books that been bringing that flame back to life.

TICE: Oh? And what do you think it is then, daughter?

CALI: I been talking to him about the Greeks...

TICE: Ah, the Greeks.

CALI: And he sings while I wash; there's been a notable improvement.

TICE: Cali. He wants one night with you. Just one night. Then he'd be gone.

CALI: I believe its more than that.

TICE: No. This is my house.

CALI: Yeah. And I make the bed you sleep in.

TICE: That man wasn't nothing but a piece of string the wind blew in when he crossed my door. I taught him the bible. I taught him Marx. He's a box man if I ever met one. I stirred that man.

CALI: So did I, father.

TICE: All right. Maybe you did. But my answer is no.

CALI: This isn't yours to say.

TICE: He's not made to love you.

CALI: Maybe not. But he makes me...wonder.

TICE: He makes you "wonder". Oh Jesus spare me.

CALI: And then something goes. Pop inside, when he makes me laugh.

TICE: He makes you "pop" inside? Huh. What are you, a piece of corn?

CALI: Don't you dare make fun of me.

TICE: There's things we don't know about him.

CALI: There's things you don't know about me.

TICE: Cali. I am saying this as your father: not now and not when he leaves this house.

CALI: So this is what you've become? No room in that head of yours left for feeling?

TICE: Feel all you want. I'm warning you not to touch.

CALI: I can't live without touchin'!

TICE: Well damn it, learn to. *(Beat)* Sometimes love.
Well.

CALI: Leave me alone. I heard you.

TICE: It's a thing you just can't take up in your arms.
Sometimes love's behind you, where you can't touch it.
Rosie, yeah, Rosie's a good woman and there's a lot of
her to touch, and one of these days I might just decide
to do some more of that touching, but behind me, still
breathing on my neck, is your mother, Isabel. And
today, that's still enough for me. Yeah, you think I'm
dried up. Got no sense left in my body. You're wrong,
girl. I've got a body 'bout as wide as an ocean. Isabel,
she plunged her hands deep in me, and when she got
finished, I was something else all together, not just for
loving her, but for loving and wanting another kind
of Alabama. No, another kind of world, one I couldn't
see, not yet. But just 'round the corner. Just 'round the
corner. *(Beat)* The way Corbin looks at you, I know that
look. And the way you look back, I know that too. But
watch out. Love like that can make you think you've
got the world fixed between the two of you. But that's
only half. You stop there, you don't use that ocean out
past this room, out past this city line, it's just gonna.
Stop being ocean. And one day you'll wake and look
out and that ocean's just an old pond out back, even
the fish have left it. *(Some moments of silence)*

CALI: I won't leave you, Father.

TICE: I'm not afraid of being left.

CALI: Then what is it?

TICE: Something's woke up inside you. But just don't
let it be him. Use what he makes you feel, but take it
somewhere else. You're breathing fire, girl, but don't
use that flame to warm his feet.

CALI: I am not a dragon! Stop turning everythin' into everythin' else. I'm not wakin' up. I never went to sleep to begin with. But like you, I once loved. Only my husband, he never talked to me. Or looked me in the face. That was my first disappointment. Then he died and I didn't miss him. That was my second disappointment for I'd sort of looked forward to finally feelin' something deep. That kinda life and folks leave you alone.

TICE: Listen to me, Cali. He's a good student. And tomorrow he'll be gone. It'll be just you and me again. Let's leave it at that. Better idea, you show me how to swing.

CALI: But Daddy—

TICE: *(Silencing her)* There's nothing more to talk about. *(He takes up the ax again.)* Haven't done this in a while. Thought I might start buildin' up my arms a bit. Long fight ahead of us. Who knows, might even get real good. Enter the competition at the county fair end of the month. *(He raises the ax.)*

CALI: First thing is, you've got to loosen that grip. You hold on too tight and it won't split the wood. That's right. But you don't do it in this house 'cause choppin' wood inside a house is the second sign of madness.

TICE: What's the first?

CALI: Entertainin' the thought that you'll ever have the finest swing in Birmingham. Which I already got. *(She takes the ax from him and leaves)*

(End Scene Four)

Scene Five

(TICE *and* CORBIN *together.* CORBIN *is agitated.* TICE *is very calm. He has an old cloth and he's wrapping a few things up in it for* CORBIN's *travel. He holds the items up for* CORBINn *to see. First, a piece of string*)

TICE: A piece of string for your travels. Never know when something might up and fall off and you have to tie it back on. (*He holds up a plate that's missing a big chunk out of it, polishes it, and puts it in the pile.*) A dinner plate. Can use it as a mirror too. (*Beat*) A piece of cheese.

CORBIN: That's not cheese.

TICE: Well, that's not its fault. But I assure you it's edible. And some bread to go with it.

CORBIN: You're a good man. I should hate you. Lots of people do.

TICE: You still might.

CORBIN: Why. Why do you think they hate you?

TICE: Don't know. Maybe 'cause we're the best kind of. Citizen. To see us makes them feel ashamed.

(TICE *ties up the bundle for* CORBIN.)

CORBIN: Shit.

(CORBIN *turns away from* TICE, *disturbed.*)

TICE: Well, you got to get through that too, Corbin.

CORBIN: Why'd you join the party in the first place? Can't be for the good times. Shot at. Beat up. Scared most of your days.

TICE: Well, justice, maybe.

CORBIN: Nah. Justice. Justice. Don't give me that. Why did Tice Hogan join the Communist party rather than walk on by and get on with his life?

TICE: Because I don't like being alone. And neither do you.

CORBIN: Damn you. Answer me.

TICE: You got a fever? You're sweatin'.

(TICE *nears* CORBIN *to touch his forehead and check his temperature but* CORBIN *jumps back like he'll be burned.*)

TICE: You that scared to leave this house?

(CORBIN *laughs nervously.*)

TICE: Want us to sit down one last time and write out your name? It's got six letters. Count. C O R B I N.

CORBIN: No.

TICE: T E E L. That's four.

CORBIN: No. I don't give a shit about ever seeing my name on a piece of paper again. You're just like a school girl. Put a ribbon in your hair. I'm sick of it. God damn it I didn't need it before, I can't use it now.

TICE: Your profanity is not a testament to your enlarged vocabulary.

CORBIN: You know what. Yeah. We're different you and me. But it's not just about tickets. You've got a roof. You've got clothes.

TICE: And two books.

CORBIN: You. You're one of those "nice" people. You think you're better than me.

TICE: I think we could work togeth-

CORBIN: *(Interrupts)* I don't want to work with you. I don't want anything with you. I just want to walk out of this house and forget it all. Forget...

TICE: —that you're no longer the same man.

CORBIN: No, forget that I ever tried to be somethin' different.

TICE: But you are different.

CORBIN: No. I'm not.

TICE: Yes. You are.

CORBIN: No. I am not.

TICE: You are.

CORBIN: You can't change a fucking stone.

TICE: A man is not a stone.

(Suddenly CORBIN'*s razor is at* TICE'*s throat.)*

CORBIN: Then I am not a man. *(Beat)* I need three names. People you know. People like you. Core of the party.

TICE: And then what?

CORBIN: Then. Well. It's nothin' personal, but I'll have to cut you. My own life depends on it.

TICE: The Iowan stooge for Tennessee Coal and Iron.

CORBIN: Only since I killed a foreman.

TICE: Suppose I should be honoured. If T C I thinks I'm better off dead, then we must be making a difference.

CORBIN: Nah. They read me out a dozen names. I just picked one I liked the sound of. I picked Tice cause it rhymes with. Lice. Easy to remember.

TICE: John Friar, Buddy Wall.

CORBIN: Christ. I didn't even have to cut you first. *(Puts the knife closer to* TICE'*s skin)* One more.

TICE: Michael Grimes.

*(*CORBIN *releases* TICE *but keeps the knife out and ready to use.)*

CORBIN: You surprised?

TICE: Nah. I knew what you were from the start. Just wasn't sure how you'd go about it.

CORBIN: Bullshit.

TICE: Oh yeah. But I thought to myself "Tice Hogan. You'll never have a chance like this at your door again. Let him in. Go to work. Perform a miracle".

CORBIN: You wanted to make me a better man.

TICE: No. That's where you're wrong. It was all about the challenge. If I could turn a snitch like you into a comrade, there wouldn't be a thing outside this house that could stop me. Not a thing. And I'd blow apart that noise inside my ear I fight every damn day that says, "Human nature doesn't change". "You can't remake the world". If I could change a man like you, Hallelujah. What's next? *(Beat)* This isn't about you. It never was about you. That's just yourself telling you lies.

CORBIN: I don't believe you.

TICE: I used you.

CORBIN: No. We were friends.

TICE: I never gave a fuck about you, Corbin Teel. I don't even like you.

CORBIN: That's a lie.

TICE: I just made a poor bet, that's all.

CORBIN: And you lost..

(TICE *just stares at* CORBIN *some moments, then he spits in his face.* CORBIN *doesn't wipe it off, just stares at* TICE.)

CORBIN: *(Quietly)* You fuckin' lost.

TICE: Yeah. I believe I did. And you know what you're doing?

CORBIN: What?

(TICE *says the following slowly, with a kind of sincerity but also with something else.*)

TICE: You are breaking my heart.

CORBIN: God damn your arrogance.

(CORBIN *attacks* TICE *and seems about to cut his throat. But suddenly* CALI *is there, at their side. She holds the ax over* CORBIN.)

CALI: You're going to kill my father, then be quick. I can't stop you. But by the time your blade is half way 'cross his throat, I'll stick my ax in yours. Don't underestimate me, Mister Teel. I cut wood. I skin rabbits. I may've been stupid enough to fall for a man like you but I can cut you out of my heart so fast it won't miss a beat.

(*After some moments,* CORBIN *releases* TICE. *He faces* CALI *and her ax.*)

CALI: Here. Take these notes with you.

(CALI *holds out to* CORBIN *a couple of printed pages, folded up. Hardly glancing at the papers,* CORBIN *takes them.*)

CALI: They'll tell your bosses more than they need to know about the inner workings of the Party. Now get out.

(CORBIN *just stands there, looking at* CALI.)

CORBIN: So. You do want me.

CALI: Yes. (*Beat*) And I hope you die.

(CORBIN *glances once at* TICE, *then he exits.* CALI *and* TICE *look at one another in silence for some moments, then:*)

TICE: Hot-doggit, girl! Those're the pages I've been missin' from my bible.

CALI: Yeah. But he don't know it.

(*End Scene Five*)

Scene Six

(It is evening. TICE *is alone. He is carrying his two books. Outside a storm is coming in.)*

TICE: Can't change human nature. That's a fact. Right. *(Suddenly in a rage, he smashes the books to the floor).* Take a look at yourselves. You're just damn books.

(After some moments, CALI *comes into the room. She is wearing the blue ribbon in her hair. She regards* TICE *in silence. She notes the books on the floor.)*

TICE: You ever notice there's a crack in the ceiling looks like a wheelbarrow.

CALI: More like the map of a city.

TICE: Or a beetle.

CALI: And see there, a row of houses. And there, a row of trees.

TICE: No birds in the sky.

CALI: Just can't see 'em. They're living in the houses. It's the folks that're hanging in the sky. *(Beat)* You gave him names. You betrayed your friends.

TICE: Yeah. I got to looking at Corbin so hard, I forgot 'bout looking ahead.

CALI: You can't go back to the Party.

TICE: No, don't think I can. I think I've lost my way.

*(*CALI *and* TICE *are silent together.)*

CALI: Daddy. Sometimes I hear you. Other times, no. Lately I've been trying not to hardest, but my ears they come awake of their own accord. Do you know what I mean?

TICE: Yesterday I'd've said: yes. So today I'll say: no.

CALI: Good. That means its my own.

TICE: Cali. Those names I gave Corbin. They're names of board members at T C I.

CALI: Did he know that?

TICE: I don't think so.

(As CALI *speaks she pulls the ribbon from her hair.)*

CALI: I met Estelle on the corner tonight. We went down to the Joy Boy Club. Danced a little. I wore this ribbon in my hair. On my way home, I saw Tucker. *(She cannot bring herself to say the words but she must.)* Daddy. Corbin's dead. T C I killed him.

*(*TICE *just stares at* CALI, *stunned.)*

TICE: How do you know?

CALI: Tucker said they found his body, just a little ways up the road. I think he was trying to make it back here.

*(*CALI *and* TICE *look at one another for a long moment.)*

TICE: I better go. Find out what kind of trouble this might bring. You be alright?

*(*CALI *nods.* TICE *begins to leave.)*

TICE: You are the apple of my eye, Cali. There's no changing that.

*(*TICE *is gone. A storm is beginning outside.* CALI *picks up the books and replaces them on the table. Then she speaks with calm measure, as though her voice had to travel a long distance to reach* CORBIN.*)*

CALI: Corbin Teel, they're saying you were a good snitch. A real good snitch. That you gave the men at T C I some names. And they laughed for a long time. You didn't know why. One of those men in the nice suits, he laughed so hard he farted. Then they stuck a knife in your side. You asked them why. They didn't even hear you, just stepped over your body and moved on. *(Beat)* Corbin Teel.

(CALI *stands in the coming storm. The rain comes down hard on the roof.)*

(End Scene Six)

Epilogue

(TICE *is ready to return to where he came from.)*

TICE: Funny thing about time is, not how it doesn't come back to you. But how it does.

I didn't leave the Party. Did for a little while. But then it got real cold. My daughter was always up and gone and she forgot to chop the wood for the fire. So I went back over to Tucker's house. He always had it roaring. And from there, all those years went flashing past us, sparked up in jail time, hiding under floor boards and always. Always. That deeply underrated phenomenon: the persistent murdering of resistance. *(Beat)* That's thirty-four letters. I still take the time to count.

Some of the things we did in those years, well, they fell apart. Some of the things, they didn't. But what lasted? Yeah, what lasted. That's always the question that finally comes to us. Shhh. There it is again. Listen. *(He makes a soft humming noise, which lasts one long breath.)* A humming that'd be felt for decades, if you knew where to put your ear to the wall, if you knew how to listen.

One in my head. One in my throat. One in the mattress. Three bullets in all.

I was asleep. It was some years after Corbin.

They were thugs for the management and they made no knock on my door. But they didn't get my daughter. Nah. Cali was out late that evening, holding a Party

meeting to unionize workers in the fields. They say
fires burn because its in their nature to burn. Yeah,
I can go with that, and that it's in the nature of the
dream of a better world to collapse at the feet of it's
tiresome dreamers. Just how it is, that's all. *(He takes an
apple from his pocket.)* Inevitable. Predictable. Yeah. But
who the hell knows the nature of the apple? Maybe it's
true nature is to swim, or to fly. Maybe the apple is a
friend. Maybe this here fruit can break your heart. *(He
holds the apple up to his ear.)* Or maybe it's a clock. Time
to go home. Time to make that fast, flying, fuck of a
trip back to forever land. *(He moves to exit, then stops.)*
Or hey, maybe an apple is a letter from another world.
The world that walks behind us. The world that won't
ever let us go.

And all you have to do. *(He takes out the knife and neatly
cuts the apple in two.)* Is open it. Read what it says on the
inside. And then, get to work. *(Now he opens the apple
and reads what the apple says on the inside.)* Well I'll be
damned.

*(TICE studies the public, then he almost smiles. He squats
and carefully puts the pieces of apple on the stage floor. He
stands up, no longer smiling at the audience, just looking
at them. Then he exits. A light lights the apple pieces, very
brightly. As though they were burning in another world.
Then the lights go out.)*

END OF PLAY

SELECT BIBLIOGRAPHY

Communist Party. *The Communist Position on the Negro Question: self-determination for the Black Belt.* New York, Workers Library, [1933?].

Davis, Mike. *Prisoners of the American Dream: Politics and Economy in the History of the U S Working Class.* Verso, 1986.

Giddings, Paula. *When and Where I Enter...: the Impact of Black Women on Race and Sex in America.* William Morrow and Company, Inc. 1984.

Hathaway, Clarence A. *Who are the friends of the Negro people?* New York, Workers Library Publishers, 1932.

Hooker, James R. *Black revolutionary; George Padmore's Path from Communism to Pan-Africanism.* London, Pall Mall Press, 1967.

Hunter, Tera W. *To 'Joy My Freedom: Southern Black Women's Lives and Labors After the Civil War.* Harvard University Press, 1998.

Kelley, Robin D. G. *Freedom Dreams: the Black Radical Imagination.* Beacon Press, 2002.

Kelley, Robin D. G. Hammer and Hoe: *Alabama Communists During the Great Depression.* Chapel Hill, 1990.

Naison, Mark. *Communists in Harlem During the Depression.* Urbana, University of Illionis Press, 1983.

Painter, Nell Irvin. *The Narrative of Hosea Hudson; His Life as a Negro Communist in the South*. Cambridge, Harvard University Press, 1979.

Rachleff, Peter, editor. *Starving Amidst Too Much and Other I W W Writings*. Charles H Kerr Publishing, 2005.

Robinson, Cedric J. *Black Marxism: the Making of the Black Radical Tradition*. Zed Books, 1983.

Roediger, David. *Working Towards Whiteness: How American's Immigrants Became White*. Basic Books, 2005.

Roediger, David. *Towards the Abolition of Whiteness*. Verso, 1994.

Shachtman, Max. *Race and Revolution*. Verso, 2003

Trotter, Joe William Jr. *Black Milwaukee: The Making of the Industrial Proletariat 1915-45*. University of Illinois Presss, 1985.

Zinn, Howard. *The Twentieth Century: a People's History*. Harper Perennial, 1998.

Made in the USA
Monee, IL
19 December 2022

22576322R00056